THE ALBIGENSIAN
OR
CATHARIST HERESY

THE ALBIGENSIAN

OR

CATHARIST HERESY

A STORY AND A STUDY

BY

EDMOND HOLMES

Author of
" *The Creed of Christ,*" " *The Creed of Buddha,*"
" *The Secret of Happiness,*" " *Dying Lights and Dawning,*" *&c.*

LONDON

WILLIAMS AND NORGATE, LTD.

14 HENRIETTA STREET, COVENT GARDEN, W.C. 2

1925

Printed in Great Britain.

CONTENTS

THE ALBIGENSIAN OR CATHARIST HERESY

CHAPTER I

DOCTRINE, PRACTICE AND GENERAL HISTORY

MOST of us who know anything about the history of Europe in the Middle Ages have heard of the Albigensian heretics in the South of France, of the crusade which Pope Innocent III launched against them in the early years of the thirteenth century and of the relentless war which Simon de Montfort, the father of our Earl Simon the Righteous, waged against them. And we have a vague idea that the Albigenses were heretics of a particularly malignant type—the erroneousness of their doctrine being only equalled by the depravity of their morals—and that therefore they richly deserved their terrible fate.

This is as much as the man of average culture knows, or imagines that he knows, about them. There are other things which he does not know, but ought to know. He does not know that the

Albigensian Crusade was the culminating, though not the final, act in a great drama which shook to its very foundations the whole fabric of Latin Christianity and produced momentous changes in the policy of the Church of Rome, the Mendicant movement, which did so much to renew the life of the Church, having been its direct outcome. Nor does he know that one of the consequences of the crusade was the destruction of " Provençal " civilization, and that another was the incorporation of Southern France in the dominions of the French King.

The word Albigensian is a misnomer, the use of which is apt to lead to a serious underestimate of both the scope and the duration of the heretical movement. We are apt to assume that the movement was confined to the first half of the thirteenth century, and to a limited region in the South of France. And it is true that it reached its maximum of intensity in the thirteenth century and in the South of France. But, far from being confined to any one locality, it overran southern and western Europe from Constantinople to the Pyrenees and from the Mediterranean to the North Sea. And, far from being confined to any one half-century, it lasted from the tenth century, when it first appeared (in Bulgaria), till towards the end of the fifteenth, when it finally died out (in Bosnia).

Albi is to-day a town of some 20,000 inhabitants in the Department of Tarn. Toulouse was the chief stronghold of the heretics, and as it has always been a far more important town than Albi, one is at a loss to understand why the latter gave its name to the heresy and the crusade. The right name for the heresy is *Catharism*, the religion of *catharsis*, or purification.

History has done less than justice to the Catharists. For history, in this matter, has been largely under the control of the Church of Rome; and the Church, having persecuted the heretics with relentless ferocity, has ever since done its best to justify its action by blackening the reputation of its victims. I know of only one work on Catharism which is both authoritative and comprehensive—Schmidt's *Histoire et Doctrine de la secte des Cathares ou Albigeois;* and my study of that work has convinced me that the popular estimate of the heretics and their heresy needs to be revised. Schmidt was a Professor of Theology at Strasbourg. His name is German, but he was a Frenchman and wrote in French. His work, which was published in Paris and Geneva in 1849, is based on a careful study of all the available documentary evidence. At the end of the first volume he gives a list of the documents, some three hundred in number, which he had consulted; and at the foot of each page he gives his authority for every statement of fact that he makes. His diligence in amassing evidence was only equalled by his impartiality in interpreting it. He had no axe of his own to grind, no thesis to establish, no dominant idea to deflect him from the path of honest research. His prejudices, if one must call them so, seem to have cancelled one another. As an Evangelical Christian, he condemned the doctrines of the heretics. As a human being, he condemned the cruelties of their persecutors.

His work, which was published seventy-six years ago, has long been out of print. It deserves to be brought up to date by a competent editor and given again to the world. As I am too old, too ignorant and too inexperienced (in these matters) to undertake so formidable a task, I will content myself with giving a brief sketch of the Catharist movement, based for the most part on Schmidt's work, but also in part on Achille Luchaire's interesting and illuminating *History of Innocent III*. The criticism of Catharist philosophy will be my own.

What did the Catharists[1] believe and teach?

[1] The heretics are sometimes spoken of collectively as *Cathari* or *Cathars*, but this name seems to belong more particularly to the ultra-ascetics who were believed to have received the gift of the Holy Spirit and who were

All their writings were destroyed by the Inquisition. It is doubtful if one survives. For our knowledge of what they taught we must therefore rely on the testimony of their enemies. As regards the main points of their teaching, this may on the whole be trusted; for on those points all historians and theologians in all the ages during which Catharism flourished and in all the countries which it invaded are unanimous.

Was Catharism a *Christian* heresy? Whatever answer may be given to this question, there can be no doubt that, in its progress through a succession of Christian countries, Catharism assimilated itself in many ways to Christianity. In order to do this it had to make a free use of the Christian creeds and Scriptures, accepting in these whatever it found it convenient to accept, and interpreting and arranging them at its good pleasure. Of the Christian Scriptures the Catharists regarded the New Testament only as authoritative. They had their own version, or versions, of it; and in their interpretation of it they seem to have subordinated the letter to the spirit whenever it suited them to do so, and conversely to have taken literally passages which are obviously figurative and parabolic. Besides

---

also known as *perfecti*. For the heresy as such and for the heretics as a body the words *Catharism* and *Catharists* seem to be more appropriate.

the New Testament, they seem to have regarded as authoritative certain apocryphal writings, especially one which set forth an alleged dialogue between Jesus and St. John.

The fundamental doctrine of Catharism is that God, being absolutely good, cannot be the author of evil, and, being eternally unchangeable, cannot be the author of what is transitory. From this they argue that he could not have created the material world, the world of our normal experience; for in that world there is much evil and no permanence; and there is also much disorder and much confusion, defects which are incompatible with the alleged providence of God. How then did the world come into being? It has not existed from all eternity, nor is it the product of blind chance. Therefore it must have been created by an evil principle or power.

In their interpretation of this doctrine the Catharists were divided into two schools,—the school of *absolute*, and the school of *modified*, *dualism*. The latter, which had at least three sub-schools, held that the Spirit of Evil had been created good and had separated himself from God of his own free will; and it differed from the school of absolute dualism in some other important respects. I need not go into these. Absolute dualism both preceded and outlived its rival, and it was also much more widely spread.

I will therefore confine myself, in this study of Catharism, to what may perhaps be regarded as the orthodox type of it. It is a significant fact that where and when Catharism was at the zenith of its power (in Languedoc, at the end of the twelfth and beginning of the thirteenth century) absolute dualism reigned without a rival. There is another reason why a separate study of modified dualism can be dispensed with : the two schools taught the same asceticism and the same morality.

In absolute dualism there is a fundamental and eternal opposition between good and evil. There are two natures eternally opposed to one another ; two masters without beginning or end ; two creators ; two Gods. One is the principle of light, the other of darkness ; one is good, the other evil ; each has his creation, his dominion, his world. The good God has created spirits, pure beings who have not fallen under the sway of the senses ; his domain is that of the higher intelligences ; his world is the spiritual world where all is perfect and good.

The bad God—known to the Catharists as the Devil, Lucifer and Luciabel—has created all things which are visible, material and transitory. He created the primitive elements, and out of these made the bodies of all things, animate and inanimate. He has not only created all these, but he also governs the world to which they belong; he is in a sense their providence; the good God has nothing to say to them. From the bad God come all the evils which afflict the world —storms, floods, droughts, famines, plagues, diseases, and catastrophes of all kinds; but we also owe to him the fecundity of animate nature and the crops which sustain life.

Above all, he is the author of all the moral evil in the world; of all that is inhuman, barbarous, and unjust in laws and social institutions; of wars, persecutions, executions, acts of revenge, and the like. As the creator of the human body he is the original cause of all sin; for sin does not belong to the spirit, is not the outcome of a weak or corrupt will, but is inherent in the matter which the bad God has created.

The world of the good God is the world of spirit and of light. He built it up out of four elements, immaterial, pure, and unchangeable. He has his own skies, his own sun, his own stars. This spiritual world has no relation whatever to the world of matter. God's concern is for his own world and for it only. He has peopled it with celestial men, each of whom has a *body*—" a spiritual body "—and a *soul*. Each of them has also a special *spirit* to take care of him and order his goings. This spirit has a celestial body of its own, and, besides being the man's guardian angel, is also, in some sort, a constituent principle of his being. The dwellers in God's world were all created at the same time, in the beginning of things, and (apart from those who "fell") have ever since lived with God in his glory. The Catharists claimed Scriptural authority for all these doctrines. In particular they claimed Pauline authority for the doctrine of body, soul and spirit.

The world which the good God created, though invisible to the dwellers on earth, and unreal, as they judge of reality, is alone visible—to those who see things as they are—and alone real. The world of the bad God is unreal, null and void.

Thus there are two Gods, two creations, two worlds. Each of these Gods has had his own revelation, the good God in the New Testament, the bad in the Old. Assuming that the true God is absolutely good, the Catharists argued that the God of the Old Testament could not be the good God. They went further. They contended that the God of the Old Testament was diametrically opposite in character to the God of the New, and that as the latter was good, the former must be bad. In support of this contention they appealed to the character of God as presented in the Old Testament, his cruelty, his vindictiveness, his injustice, his destructiveness, his institution of the *lex talionis* and the barbarous rite of circum-

cision. They also appealed to his dealings with
Adam and Eve. When he forbade them to eat
the fruit of a certain tree, either he knew that
they would eat it, in which case he was tempting
them to their ruin; or he did not know, in which
case he was not omniscient. That Jehovah was
the bad God was one of their fundamental dogmas.
It was not the good God, but the bad, who gave
the Law to Moses, and ordered the goings of the
people of Israel. It follows that the Law, not
having been given by the good God, is all false-
hood and vanity, and leads, not to salvation,
but to death. It is false, because instead of
enjoining universal love, it allows men to hate
their enemies. Hence its abolition by Christ,
which alone suffices to prove that it was the work
of the bad God. If it had been intrinsically
good it could never have been superseded.

If the bad God created the bodies only of men,
and the good God the souls only, how did the
latter come to be imprisoned in the former and
so, instead of remaining pure and holy, come
under the domination of sin and evil? This
question is, of course, unanswerable. Logic
demands that there should be no intercourse
whatever between the two worlds. But experience tells us that there is such intercourse, in
the person of man, who has a foot, so to speak,
in each world. This fact is fatal to the theory

of two parallel worlds. But, rather than admit this, the Catharists, in their attempt to account for man's dual nature, had recourse to the desperate expedient of a fantastic myth : The bad God, beholding with envious eyes the happiness of the good God and his people, introduced himself into heaven as an angel of incomparable beauty and splendour, and won the affection of some of the souls that dwelt there, attracting them so strongly that at last they consented to follow him to earth and separate themselves from the good God. The good God seems to have allowed them to depart, and to have decided that, as they had exiled themselves from their spiritual home, they should endure the punishment of their sin by remaining on earth in their material bodies, and there, by repentance and a reformed life, qualifying themselves for readmission to heaven.

It follows from this myth that there are two natures in man, the spirit which attaches the soul to the good God, and the body which attaches it to the bad God. It follows also that there was no one first man from whom all men are descended, and that there has been no continuous creation of souls by God. The earth is peopled to-day by the souls that followed the bad God to earth; and, according to Catharist doctrine, their number, whatever it may have

B

originally been, decreases steadily as souls are
purified and return to heaven. The Catharists
also believed that the bad God found human
bodies for some of his own demons. These are
the monsters of cruelty, tyranny and wickedness
generally whom one sometimes meets in human
form.

The soul of man is of celestial origin. It is
out of its element in the material world. Why
does the good God allow it to remain there?
In order, as I have said, to punish it for its disobedience. Earth, the domain of the bad God,
is a place of punishment and penitential suffering. It is the true hell and the only hell. But it
is a place of purgatorial, not of eternal punishment. The souls of men will not remain in it
for ever. They will all be " saved," they will
all return to heaven. Predestination to life, not
to life *or* to death (as taught by St. Augustine
and his descendants in the line of religious
thought) is the everlasting purpose of God. If
God could pick and choose among the souls which
he has created, destining some to salvation and
others to perdition, he would no longer be the
good God; he would be more unjust and more
treacherous than the bad God. Apart from
those which have been created by the bad God,
there will be no lost souls.

If all the souls which the good God created are

predestined to eternal life, there is no need for a saviour, in the orthodox sense of the word. Nevertheless the Catharists found a place, and an all-important place, in their system for the person of Jesus Christ. They said that God sent him to earth to save the souls of men, not by dying for them, but by unfolding to them their origin and their destiny, and showing them how best to accomplish their work of penitential purgation.

Though the Catharists called Jesus the " Son of God " they did not think of him as God. He is a creature—inferior to the Creator. Nor, though he lived and worked on earth, was he ever incarnate as man. The doctrine of the incarnation of God would naturally be abhorrent to the Catharists. Jesus took the *form* of a man while on earth, but his spirit was never imprisoned in matter. The Holy Ghost was regarded as being, next to Jesus, the chief of all the celestial spirits; but the Catharists also applied the epithet *holy* to each of the guardian spirits of the celestial souls. When the souls of men have accomplished their penitential work, the guardian spirits, who had watched over them in heaven, are restored to them, and each of these spirits becomes the Paraclete or Consoler of the soul to which it is attached, as long as the latter has to remain on earth.

In support of their myth the Catharists appealed freely to the texts in the Bible which seemed to countenance their doctrines; and they also made use of the terms and formulas of Christian theology in order to give expression to theories which were in reality foreign to Christian orthodoxy. All their efforts were directed towards making their dualistic system pass as genuine Christianity. But in truth it differed profoundly from the Christianity of the Church. Christ, as the Catharists conceived of him, was not the Saviour but the Teacher of mankind. The earth-bound souls would be saved in any case, so they had no need of a Saviour. But they had need of a Teacher if they were to shorten their stay on earth. The work of Christ was to reveal to them their nature and their origin, to make them realize that they were under the sway of a false God, to show them the path of penitential purification which would lead them to the true God, and to form a society— the Church—of all who were prepared to accept his (Christ's) revelation and submit to his laws.

The Catharists claimed that their Church was carrying on the work of Christ, and that only by joining it could men enter the path of penitential purification and so shorten their stay on earth. But how about the souls of those who died before Christ came? The Catharists met this difficulty by teaching, what in any case they were bound to teach, the doctrine of rebirth. If there was an original Fall, as the result of which a definite number of souls fell from heaven to earth, and if there has since been no addition to that number, it is only by the action of the law of rebirth that the earth has continued to be inhabited by mankind. The departed soul is reborn in another body, reborn again and again, until the time comes for its final deliverance from earth. The Catharists carried belief in rebirth so far as to hold that sinful and impenitent souls could be temporarily imprisoned in the bodies of animals, or at least of quadrupeds and birds.

From doctrine let us pass on to practice. The aim of Catharism, as a practical scheme of life, was to detach man by every possible means from the material world, to break the bonds which bind him to earth. As matter is the creation of the Devil,[1] all voluntary contact with it is to be avoided as impurity. This postulate is the supreme law of Catharist morality.

What is sin? The original act of sin—yielding to the seductions of the Devil—seems to have perverted the nature of the celestial soul, a perversion which shows itself in love of the things of earth; and sin now takes the form of preferring

[1] I may as well call the bad God by the name with which we are all familiar.

the world of the Devil, with its false and transitory interests, to the higher world which is alone real and true.

All sins are potentially mortal, but no sin is actually mortal unless it manifests itself in an act. The moral precepts of the Catharists were all prohibitions, most of which were of an extremely rigorous nature. Taken all together they constituted an asceticism even more severe than that which the Catholic Church imposes on those who aspire to the highest degree of religious perfection. Besides the sins which the Catholic Church counts as mortal, such as murder, robbery, adultery and the rest, the following were counted as mortal sins by the Catharists and strictly forbidden to all who wished to lead a spiritual life :

(1) The possession of property. Absolute poverty was to be the rule of life.

(2) Communication with those who were still attached to the world, except indeed in order to convert them. All ties of friendship and relationship were to be broken.

(3) Disloyalty to truth. The truth was always to be told with absolute frankness and at whatever cost. Swearing, in the sense of taking an oath, was a mortal sin. " Let your yea be yea, and your nay, nay."

(4) The shedding of human blood for any purpose or on any pretext. The soldier who killed an enemy in battle, the judge who sentenced a criminal to death, and—above all—the priest who delivered a heretic to the secular power, were as culpable as murderers and assassins.

(5) The killing of animals other than reptiles and fishes.

(6) The eating of the flesh of animals.

(5 and 6 were practical deductions from the doctrine of metempsychosis.)

(7) The last and gravest of all mortal sins was that of sexual intercourse. Even marriage was strictly forbidden. For sexual intercourse, besides involving the gratification of a carnal lust, was the means devised by the Devil for the propagation of the human race and the consequent perpetuation of his own empire.

How did the soul obtain pardon for its sins and deliverance from the power of the Devil? Here the Catharists departed entirely from the teaching of orthodox Christianity. Neither the death of Christ on the cross nor the good works of the penitent counted for anything in the eyes of God. What was needed for the remission of sin was an absolute change of life. The penitent must

renounce the world and enter the Catharist
Church, the only Church which could give men
the assurance and the means of salvation.
Reception into the Church was effected by a
solemn act which was not symbolical only but also
sacramental. This act was baptism, not the
baptism of water, which the Catharists rejected
as having been instituted by the Devil, but the
baptism of the Holy Spirit, which, as they
claimed, had been instituted by Christ. The
baptism of the Holy Spirit was accomplished by
means of the laying on of hands, a ceremony to
which they gave the name of the *consolamentum*.
This baptism caused the Holy Spirit to descend
upon the soul; in other words, it reunited the soul
to the guardian spirit from which its fall had
separated it, but which would henceforth be its
" Comforter " or Consoler till its body died and
its pilgrimage on earth was ended.

When a man had received the *consolamentum*
and, with it, the Holy Spirit and deliverance from
the power of matter and its creator, he was
regarded as *Perfect*—that is, as wholly cleansed
from the guilt and taint of sin. It is to these
Perfecti, or " Perfect Ones," that the name
Catharus—(he who has been cleansed or purified)
—properly belongs. Other names by which
they were familiarly known were the *Good
Christians*, the *Good, Kind men* (" les Bons-

hommes ") and the *Friends of God*. They were also sometimes spoken of as the *Comforters* or *Paracletes*. In the eyes of the Catholic leaders, who feared and hated them, they were the heretics *par excellence ;* and they were always known to them by that name.

The glorious privilege which the *perfecti* believed themselves to have won back, far from authorizing them to spend their days in mystical contemplation, imposed on them stern obligations and a severe asceticism. They were bound to go from place to place, to preside at religious meetings, to preach and to teach, to exhort the faithful to remain steadfast during the stress of persecution, and to give the *consolamentum* to all whom they judged worthy to receive it. They wished to be true successors of the Apostles and our Lord, and to imitate them in their privations and sufferings as well as in their ceaseless labours for the spread of the Gospel. They did not allow themselves to possess any personal property ; the whole of their possessions and indeed the whole of their existence they dedicated to the service of the Church. Their life was a series of fasts and privations ; it was regulated by the solemn undertaking which they made when they were received into the circle of the Elect. Not only did they renounce all the ties and joys of family life, but they also made a vow of poverty and self-abnegation. They lived on the bread and fruit and fish which were offered them by the faithful. Thrice in each year they fasted for forty days; and they also fasted thrice in each week. During their fasts they lived on nothing but bread and water.

There were women among them; but these did not go from place to place as the men did; nor did they preach the Gospel. Some of them led solitary lives; others led a communal life, occupying themselves with manual work, with the education of young girls and with the care of the sick and the poor. They were allowed in extreme cases to administer the *consolamentum*; and they were also allowed in certain exceptional cases to relax the rigour of their rule of life and go back into the world, but only on the understanding that they would receive the *consolamentum* before they died.

The *perfecti* were held in the utmost veneration by the members of their sect, and in general by the people among whom they led their austere and simple life. When they arrived at a village or a castle every one hastened to welcome them, and offer them food and other necessaries of life. The nobles counted it an honour to wait on them at table; they provided them with horses and armed escorts, and in times of danger conducted them to places of safety even at the risk of their own lives. They also made them presents and bequests of money for the benefit of their community. The preaching of the *perfecti* was listened to with the closest attention; their advice was respected and followed; and they exercised an influence to which all classes were ready to submit. When they met one of the faithful or entered his house their blessing was asked for, and when given was received with profound reverence.

But their rule of life imposed a strain on human nature which few men could be expected to bear. One of the authorities whom Schmidt quotes says that in his time, about 1240, there were only 4,000 *perfecti* in the whole of Europe. A generation earlier, before the Albigensian crusade, the number must have been larger than this, but it could never have been large.

If there were few *perfecti*, there were many *credentes*, or believers. And at one time there seems to have been a lower grade called *auditores*, or hearers, a name given to those who were receiving their first instruction in the Catharist faith. Many things were permitted to the believers which the *perfecti* denied to themselves. They might marry, possess property, make war, and eat and drink what they pleased, but they had to confess their sins to the ministers of their sect. They were not all equally initiated into the mysteries of the Catharist faith. What was impressed on all of them was that outside the Catharist Church there was no salvation and that therefore they must some day or other receive the *consolamentum*. This might be deferred till the approach of death; but those who died " unconsoled " would have to be born again in the flesh and continue their penitential pilgrimage on earth. Those who were grievously wounded or seriously ill were as eager to receive the *consolamentum* as any Catholic who was dying would be to receive absolution from a priest. But the Catharists who were in danger of death had to promise, before they received the *consolamentum*, that if they recovered they would lead the severely ascetic life of the *perfecti ;* and there were cases in which the *consolamentum* was refused to those whose desire for it was not thought to be sincere.

Why was the reception of the *consolamentum* put off, as a rule, till the approach of death ? One reason was that after its reception there might be no opportunity for a relapse into sin. In the fourth century A.D. Constantine the Great and other converts to Christianity put off their baptism till the eve of death, in the belief that the baptismal rite would cleanse them from all the sins that they had ever committed. And to-day the Catholic who confesses and is absolved on his death-bed believes that his salvation is thereby assured. But there was a special reason why the Catharist should defer the reception of the *consolamentum* till he was in the shadow of death. The obligation to lead a severely ascetic life was one which he was not prepared to meet. He is not to be blamed for this. Rigorous asceticism of the Catharist type would have incapacitated him for his work in the world. But his faith in the efficacy of the *consolamentum* was unbounded. In hopeless cases, after it had been received, rather than run the risk of a spiritual relapse, the dying Catharists, by their own action—*e.g.*, by refusing to take nourishment—sometimes accelerated the approach of death. Catharists also claimed the right, in times of violent persecution, to take their own lives, after they had received the *consolamentum*, rather than fall into the hands of the Inquisitors, who would probably have sent them to the stake.

The Catharists claimed that theirs was the only true Christian Church. Membership of the Church was confined to those who had received the Holy Spirit and were leading pure and sinless lives. The impious, the unbeliever, the evil doer were shut out from it. Catharists reproached the Catholic Church for admitting sinners of all kinds into its fold. They also reproached it for its want of charity, for the

cruelty with which it persecuted dissentient
opinion, and in general for the harshness of its
rule. They reproached it for the pomp, the
wealth and the moral laxity of its prelates, and
for the honour which was paid them by " the
world." They reproached it for its avarice, its
ambition and its love of power. These, they said,
are the fruits which the tree has borne, and by
which we may know that it is not what it pre-
tends to be, the true Church of Christ.

The Catharist mode of worship was simplicity
itself. Catholic worship, with its imposing
temples, its excess of ornamentation and its
elaborate ceremonial, was a departure—so
Catharists contended—from the primitive purity
of the Christian Church. God was omnipresent
and might be worshipped anywhere and in any
surroundings. Catharist services were held in
castles or in hovels, in forests, in meadows,
in valleys, in caverns. When they enjoyed
powerful protection, as in Southern France
before the Albigensian crusade, and were free
from molestation, the Catharists had houses of
prayer in which they met for purposes of worship.
But those houses had no statues, pictures or
other ornaments. The altar was a table covered
with a white cloth, on which rested a New Testament open at the first chapter of the Gospel of
St. John. Statues they regarded as idols, and

the veneration of them as idolatry; and, far from venerating the cross as a sacred symbol, they held it in horror as the instrument of the suffering and humiliation of Christ, and resented its use in places of worship as recalling a triumph of the Evil One.

The service which was held in the house of prayer or other place of worship was quite simple. The minister, or, in his absence, one of the *perfecti*, read a passage from the New Testament, explaining it and bringing out the points on which the teaching of the Church of Rome seemed to be at variance with that of the Gospel. Then followed a ceremony which was called the Benediction and is sufficiently described by its name. Then the whole assembly recited the Lord's Prayer. This, as the Catharists contended, was the only prayer which Christians were authorized to use, whether in public or private. Prayer was to be addressed to God alone, the invocation of saints being regarded as irrational and unscriptural; and as God knows all our needs, the multiplication of prayers to him was considered unnecessary. When the Lord's Prayer had been recited the minister said, " Let us adore the Father, the Son and the Holy Spirit," and the congregation replied, " The grace of our Lord Jesus Christ be with us all."

The ceremony of Benediction was one to which

Catharists attached great importance. Wherever
there was freedom of worship it took place daily,
morning and evening, thus taking the place of
the matins and vespers of Catholicism.

The *consolamentum* was, as we have seen, a
baptism, not of water, but of the Holy Spirit
and of fire. The minister laid his hands on the
recipient and prayed that he might receive the
Holy Spirit. The outward act, the laying on
of hands, had no efficacy. It was the prayer
that counted. Hence it was that the virtue of
the rite depended on the moral state of the
minister. If he had sinned and lost the Holy
Spirit his prayer would have no effect. The rite
was usually administered by one of the ministers
of the sect, and it was a rule that another should
be present. But it might, if necessary, be
administered by an " unordained " *perfectus*,
or even, in special cases, by a woman. The
recipient had to be an adult in full possession
of his senses and faculties. He must have been
under strict observation for some time, for the
efficacy of the rite depended in part on his own
spiritual state. And he must have prepared
himself for the rite by prayer and by three days
of complete abstinence from food.

In normal times the *consolamentum* was
administered publicly in the presence of believers
who had come from far and wide to take part

in the service. But in times of persecution it was administered at night and in secret places, so that it might escape the cognizance of the persecutors, for he who had received the *consolamentum* was regarded by the Catholic Church as an obdurate heretic, and if he fell into the hands of the Inquisitors he had nothing to hope for but death at the stake. The service, whether held publicly or in secret, was a most solemn one. The recipient, on bended knee, promised to devote himself thenceforth to God and his gospel, to eschew lying and swearing, to lead a chaste and ascetic life, and never, even when threatened with a cruel death, to betray his faith. When the service was over he had to retire into solitude for forty days, during which he was to live on bread and water, and meditate on the grace which he had received and on the solemn obligation which he had undertaken for the rest of his life. When the *consolamentum* was administered to the dying, it was considered essential that the recipient should know what he was doing and be able to speak distinctly, so that he might say the necessary prayers and make the necessary promises. If any exception was ever made to this rule it was in the case of warriors who had been mortally wounded when fighting in defence of their faith.

In the *Breaking and Blessing of Bread* Cathar-

c

ism made its nearest approach to the Christian
rite of *Holy Communion*.   As bread is a product
of earth and therefore of the Evil One, the formal
blessing of it was scarcely in keeping with strict
Catharist doctrine.   A mystically metaphysical
interpretation of the rite was no doubt forthcoming; but over-subtle distinctions do not
appeal to simple minds, and the fragments of
consecrated bread which were distributed seem
to have been regarded with superstitious reverence.   In times of persecution, when the Catharist
ministers were in hiding, the blessing of bread
took place at solemn festivals only, such as
Christmas or Easter; fragments of the bread so
blessed were then carried by faithful messengers
to the towns and villages and distributed among
the believers, who carefully preserved them in
caskets, sometimes for years at a time.   But
though the bread which had been blessed was
held in such high honour, the Catharists would
have been false to their own first principles
had they identified it in any sense, whether
mystical or metaphysical, with the actual body
of Christ.   The doctrine of Transubstantiation,
which, though not yet formally defined by the
Catholic Church, was at that time beginning to
crystallize into a dogma,[1] was one which they
denied and abhorred.

[1] The Eucharistic controversy, which was carried on
with vigour and acrimony for some centuries, was not

Though the Catharists rejected the Catholic sacrament of Confession, they practised confession in public as a solemn rite and received from their ministers assurance that God had forgiven their sins. Mortal sins were confessed by the sinners individually; venial sins by one member of the congregation on behalf of the rest. This ceremony took place once a month and formed part of the regular services of the Church. The *perfecti* confessed their venial sins to one another. Such sins, if duly repented of, did not entail the loss of the Holy Spirit. Though the doctrine of " reparation " was one which the Catharists rejected, they were in the habit of imposing penances on the penitents in the form of fasts and other external observances.

In principle the Catharists condemned the practice of consecrating certain days to the worship of God. They had, however, preserved some of the great feasts of the Christian Church, especially Christmas, Easter and Pentecost. At Christmas they celebrated the descent of Christ into this wicked world. At Easter, his triumph over the Prince of this world. At Pentecost, the foundation of the Catharist Church, the Church of the Holy Spirit. Christmas and Easter were each preceded, and Pente-

---

finally closed till A.D. 1215, when the word *transubstantiation* was adopted and the doctrine defined by the Fourth Council of Lateran.

cost was followed, by a fast of about forty days, the last week of which was very rigorous.

Strictly speaking, the *perfecti*, those who had received and not forfeited the gift of the Holy Spirit, were the only members of the Catharist Church. The *credentes*, or believers, were waiting, as it were, at the portal of the Church, but had not yet been admitted into it. But as they had left the Church of Rome, and were seeking admission to the true Church, and were in close communion with the *perfecti*, they might be said to have formed, with the latter, an outward and visible Church—the body, so to speak, of which the inward and invisible Church was the soul. This outward and visible Church had its own constitution, its own organization, its own ministry.

The first condition for admission to the Catharist ministry was moral uprightness, absolute purity of life. The mission of the ministry was to communicate to the believers the gift of the Holy Spirit, and no one who had forfeited that gift could communicate it to others. The Catholic doctrine that priests who were living in mortal sin could duly administer the sacraments was one which the Catharists vehemently repudiated; and they regarded the laxity of morals in the Catholic priesthood, of which that doctrine was the outcome, as a proof of the apostasy and degeneration of the Church.

In the Catharist ministry two orders only were recognized—*bishops* and *deacons*. The bishops took precedence in all ceremonies and at all gatherings of the faithful. They ordained the deacons, gave absolution for mortal sins and presided at the meetings of the *perfecti* and their friends and protectors. Each bishop had two understudies, a senior and a junior. When a bishop died the junior understudy appointed the senior as his successor. The newly appointed bishop then raised the junior to the rank of senior; and a new junior was elected by the *perfecti* of the diocese and ordained by the bishop. The ceremony of ordination was very simple, and there is no evidence that it was supposed to confer supernatural powers on the ordained. In France and Italy, in the thirteenth century, a change was made in the mode of consecrating bishops. Before his death a bishop ordained his senior understudy as co-adjutor bishop; and on his death the latter succeeded the former as a matter of course. When the number of believers was exceptionally large there were sub-deacons as well as deacons. And as all ministers without exception were *perfecti*, and as purity of heart and life was the one essential qualification for the ministry, the lower rank could in cases of emergency discharge all the functions of the higher.

The Catharist Church was divided into dioceses, each of which was sub-divided into diaconates. The dioceses corresponded as a rule to those of the Catholic Church. The division of the dioceses into diaconates was made with great care; and such difficulties as arose in the delimitation and administration of the latter were settled by diocesan synods, composed of ministers and *perfecti*.

In the thirteenth century the Catharist communities were broken up by the Inquisitors, and their members were scattered far and wide. But even in those days the utmost care was taken to nominate bishops for all the pre-existing dioceses. The deacons and the diaconates seem to have disappeared little by little; but the place of the former was taken by leaders called *Ancients* —*perfecti* whose venerable age and steadfastness during persecution gave them an authority which their brethren gladly recognized, and who, though not ordained for the purpose, discharged all the functions of deacons.

Had the Catharist Church a supreme bishop or Pope? Some writers say that it had. According to one document there was a Catharist Pope at Constantinople, according to another, in Bulgaria. As against this positive evidence, we may set a mass of negative evidence which seems to be overwhelmingly strong. In the writings of those who were most intimately acquainted with the Catharist movement there is no mention of a heretical Pope. Among the measures taken by the Catholic Church against the heretics, and renewed again and again, not one was directed against a supreme head of their sect. In the protocols of the Inquisition in France and Italy, among the many questions addressed to accused persons and witnesses not one has any reference to the existence of such a head. Nor is his existence hinted at in any of the numerous documents which relate to the Catharist movement in Slav countries. Such unanimity of silence may surely be regarded as conclusive.

Many ecclesiastical writers in different ages and different countries have reproached the Catharists, not so much with general laxity of morals, as with having, at their secret meetings, practised revolting immoralities and blasphemous rites. The answer to these charges is that not one of the authors who have given us a detailed and quasi-authoritative account of the Catharist system has alluded to such practices, though had there been any ground for those odious charges they would naturally have made the most of them in order to add force to their arguments against the errors of Catharism. Some of the most vehement adversaries of the Catharists pay reluctant homage to the austerity of their morals. It is true that they tax them with hypocrisy, alleging that they led pure and ascetic lives in order the more surely to seduce people from the truth. But if their enemies regarded their virtues as proofs of " heretical depravity," the witness that they bore to those virtues is not invalidated by their misinterpretation of the motives that swayed them. Testimony is borne by many Catholic writers to the honesty and uprightness of the Catharists in the ordinary affairs of life, to the sincerity of their convictions, to their sobriety, to their simple way of living. Their piety, their devotion to their religion and the strictness with which they discharged their religious duties were even held up as examples to Catholics.

If further proof were needed of the baselessness of the charges that were brought against them, it would be found in the courage and constancy with which they endured relentless persecution, in the hardships and privations to which they cheerfully submitted rather than betray their faith, in the heroism—amounting in some cases to exultant joy—with which they faced the cruel death at the stake.

That slanderous charges should have been brought against them is no matter for wonder. Similar charges were brought against the early Christians when they were a despised and persecuted sect. In times of persecution a religious community has to hold its meetings where and when it can—in remote and secret places, and in the sheltering darkness of night. Meetings which are held at midnight in unknown places are necessarily surrounded with an atmosphere of mystery; and in that atmosphere curiosity readily changes into suspicion, and ignorance gives rise to all kinds of uncharitable conjectures. And if the community happens to be held up by high authority to obloquy and hatred, it is but natural that fantastically slanderous rumours should get into circulation, growing more fantastic and more slanderous as they passed from mouth to mouth. To the slanders which assailed the Catharists the Inquisitors might be expected to lend willing ears; and we can only wonder that in the more authoritative documents dealing with Catharism, charges of blasphemous rites and revolting obscenities find no place.

The charge of avarice which was sometimes brought against the Catharists can be refuted with equal ease. The Catharist believers led active and useful lives, and their industry, whether in town or country, may have enabled them to amass a certain amount of wealth. But those who did amass wealth were expected to give freely to their Church, so as to provide for the support of the *perfecti*, who had voluntarily pauperized

themselves, and for the relief of the sick and poor.
A Church which has no endowments has to depend
for its financial ways and means on contributions
from the faithful, and a Church which is liable
to be persecuted has to provide, in times of
security and comparative affluence, for its maintenance in times of adversity and destitution.
The charities of the Catharists to their own sick
and poor were often commented on by their
adversaries; and while some of these reproached
them with having confined their charities to their
own sick and poor, others accused them of having
tried by their charities to make converts of the
Catholic poor. That the Catharist Church
received considerable gifts and legacies from its
wealthy supporters, and that in some cases
collections were made by it on a large scale, is
undeniable; but whatever was received was
placed in a common chest and administered by
the bishops for the benefit of the Church as a
whole—for charitable purposes, for the support
of exiles and refugees and for carrying on the
propagandist activities which were enjoined by
their religion. I need not go into the details
of that propagandist work. Suffice it to say
that what weighed most with those whom the
Catharists sought to proselytize were the purity
and simplicity of their lives, especially as con-
trasted with those of the Catholic priests and

prelates, the constancy with which they endured persecution and their charitable care of the sick and poor.

I will now give a brief sketch of the history of Catharism, which will prepare the way for the tragic story of its rise and fall in Southern France. The founder of Catharism, if there was any one founder, is unknown; nor do we know at what place or in what year it came into being; but it is practically certain that it was born and died in the Balkan Peninsula, Bulgaria having been its cradle and Bosnia its last stronghold.

The quarrels for supremacy in the Balkan Peninsula between the Pope and the Patriarch, the anti-Latin sentiments of the people, and the lingering paganism of races which had but recently been converted, and had not yet been fully converted, to Christianity, combined to produce an atmosphere favourable to the spread of heretical ideas.

In 862 the Greek monks Methodius and Cyrillus converted the Slavs of Bulgaria to Christianity and baptized their King, Bogoris. But Bogoris, hoping to find in Latin support a counterpoise to the ascendancy of the Greek Emperor, asked the Pope to send missionaries to complete the Christianization of Bulgaria. The Pope, Nicholas I, hastened to comply with this request.

His action gave rise to a quarrel between Rome and Constantinople, which was long and violent, and, reviving in the eleventh century, led to the schism between the Western and the Eastern Churches. While the quarrel was in progress religion naturally suffered in the country over which the two Churches were fighting, and a spirit of opposition to ecclesiastical authority grew up among the people. Taking advantage of this state of things the Paulicians [1] in Armenia sent missionaries to Bulgaria in order to convert the people to their own dualistic religion.

One circumstance which contributed to the spread of heretical doctrine among the Slavs was the opposition of the Pope and the Latin missionaries to the use of the national language—or languages—in religious worship. The enforced use of an entirely foreign language, and the persecution of those who clung to their own mode of worship, exasperated the people and produced a feeling of general hostility to Rome and its teaching. The monasteries, in particular, were focuses of resistance to Latin influences and the Latin tongue. In their isolation the monks

[1] The Paulicians were a quasi-Christian sect which flourished for many centuries in Asia Minor and Armenia and had numerous adherents. While retaining some of the features of primitive Christianity they seem to have borrowed from Manichæism the dualism of its philosophy and the austerity of its ethics.

gave themselves up to speculation, which led in some cases to anti-orthodox conclusions,—conclusions which were accepted the more readily because orthodoxy was taught by an unpopular priesthood in a foreign tongue.

Meanwhile the conversion of the Slavs to Christianity was making slow progress. Even in the tenth century the pagans were still numerous, and pagan beliefs seem to have mingled themselves with Christian doctrines. Prior to their contact with Christianity the pagans had worshipped one paramount God and a number of lesser deities. But the Christian belief in the Devil, the supreme principle of evil and the arch-enemy of God and man, seems to have made a deep impression on them; and they raised this sinister personage to the rank of a deity, under the name of *Diabol*, placed him by the side of their own good God, and, regarding him as the author of all evils, moral and physical, worshipped him in the hope of averting his wrath.

Such were the circumstances in which the Catharist heresy made its appearance, probably in the early part of the tenth century, among the Slavs of the Balkan Peninsula. It is possible, as Schmidt conjectures, that it originated in some Greco-Slav monastery in Bulgaria, in which Manichæan memories still survived. The Mani-

chæan heresy, with its demand for rigorous
asceticism, made a special appeal to monastic
recluses, and it seems to have lingered on in the
monasteries of Eastern Christendom, as an
influence, if not as a formal creed, long after it
had been officially condemned and suppressed.
But, however Catharism may have originated, it
is probable that it owed its success as a proselytizing religion partly to its having been taught to
the Slav peoples in their mother tongues, partly
to its being a departure from Latin orthodoxy,
partly to its having fallen into line with the
dualistic teaching of the Pauline missionaries
and with the crude dualism which the Slav
pagans had in some sort borrowed from Christianity, partly to the novelty, the simplicity
and the intelligibility of its teaching, partly
to the appeal that it made to man's higher
nature—to his capacity for self-sacrifice and self-
denial.

From its early days, Catharism made rapid
progress both eastward and westward. The
Slavs, who took an active interest in commerce, introduced it into all the countries with
which they traded. In the eleventh century
it had adherents in Macedonia, Thrace, Asia
Minor and the principal cities of Greece. It had
also spread through Bosnia and Dalmatia into
Italy, and thence into France, and through

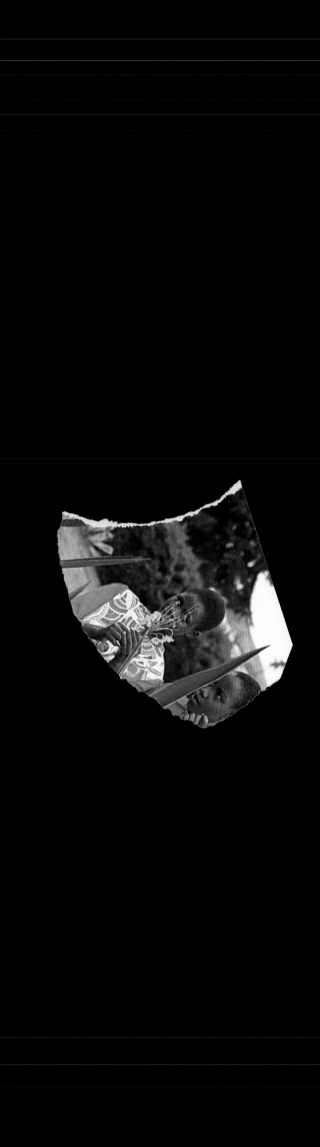

Hungary into Germany. As it moved westward it became more practical and less speculative than it had been in its origin or than it continued to be in the East. Severe asceticism and active hostility to the hierarchy and the usages of the Latin Church became its leading characteristics, and speculations as to the origin of the world retired into the background. It was not till the beginning of the twelfth century that it developed into a complete system of faith and conduct. About the same time the modified dualism which had long had a following in the Greco-Slav world invaded the Western countries and took its place by the side of absolute dualism, which, however, remained to the end the dominant creed.

In Italy Catharism found a soil prepared for its reception. There the Manichæan heresy had maintained itself for many centuries in spite of all the efforts of Popes and Emperors to extirpate it. In the time of Gregory the Great the heretics were so numerous that the Pope found it necessary to exhort the Italian bishops to take strong measures against them. After that we lose sight of them; but the heretical poison may well have survived the open profession of Manichæan doctrine and continued to propagate itself in secret. Other anti-Roman influences were at work in Italy. The Lombards in the North,

who long remained Arians, had a profound
aversion for the authority, whether Imperial or
Papal, which was seated in Rome; and even
after they had been converted to Catholicism
the name Roman was for them the synonym of
everything that was corrupt and base.   More
than once the Popes had to invoke the aid of the
Kings of the Franks against them; but the
victories won at their expense did but intensify
their hatred of Rome.   This spirit of opposition
found a further support in the growing spirit
of freedom, which had expressed itself in the
municipal institutions of the cities of Lombardy.
The ignorance, the avarice and the immorality
of the Italian clergy exposed them to the contempt of the laity and inclined the latter to lend
willing ears to anti-orthodox doctrine.   And,
with the awakening of the humanistic spirit
in Italy at the end of the eleventh century, came
a readiness to welcome and propagate ideas which
had the charm of novelty, besides being free
from the odious associations which orthodox
Catholicism had contracted.

It was about the year 1030 that Catharism
made its first public appearance in Italy.   Its
headquarters were at the castle of Monteforte
near Turin, and it counted among its supporters
many nobles who resented the exactions and
injustices of their feudal lord, the Archbishop

of Milan. The Archbishop organized a strong
expedition against the castle, and captured it
after several assaults. A large batch of heretics
who were found in it were sent to Milan, and given
their choice between recantation and the stake.
Most of them chose the latter.

Thenceforth we lose sight of Catharism in
Italy till about the middle of the twelfth century,
when we find it firmly established in the cities
of Lombardy, with a strong organization which
could not have been evolved if the doctrine had
not rooted itself deeply in the hearts and minds
of the people.

Its subsequent downfall was due, not to
persecution, though it had its full share of that,
but to the intermingling of politics and religion,
which was characteristic of public life in Italy,
especially in the twelfth and thirteenth centuries.
In the triangular contest which was carried on
for many generations with extreme bitterness
and violence, each of the combatants—the Pope,
the Emperor and the Lombard cities—regarded
the heretics as counters in the game of intrigue
and ambition, and dealt with them accordingly.
No worse fate could have befallen them. A
heresy which is taken up out of hatred for the
champions of orthodoxy, or as a stick wherewith
to beat an enemy, and which is alternately
patronized and persecuted by political rivals

D

for political ends, can scarcely be expected to
keep a lasting hold on the hearts of the people.
And a heresy which finds its advantage in a state
of moral and spiritual anarchy will in the long
run lose more than it gains by the disorders from
which it profits. The Church of Rome, the
acknowledged champion of Christian orthodoxy,
with the prestige which had accrued to it from
centuries of undisputed supremacy, with its
elaborate and far-reaching organization, with the
tentacles of its influence intertwining themselves with the social and political constitution of
every Christian State, could outlive the disorders
and scandals of that period. A heresy which
owed to those very disorders the chief political
support that it received could not. In the early
part of the fourteenth century, Catharism in
Italy was on its death-bed.

Let us go back three centuries. In the early
part of the eleventh century Catharism spread
westward from Italy. Missionary enthusiasts
of both sexes carried it in secret from place to
place, and it found followers in the country as
well as in the towns. In Southern France, in
particular, it made rapid progress. Here, as in
Italy, the soil had been prepared for it. In this,
the most civilized and cultured part of the
Western Empire, opposition to superstitious
practices, such as the worship of saints and the

adoration of relics, manifested itself in the fifth
and sixth centuries, and with this hostility to
tendencies which were associated with religious
orthodoxy were mingled the memories of heresies
which had once flourished but had been forcibly
extirpated, of Arianism, which for two centuries
had been the dominant religion of the Visigoths
of Aquitania, and had maintained itself in the
province of Narbonne long after the Kings of the
Visigoths had become Catholics; and of Priscil-
lianism, a blend of Manichæan and Gnostic
doctrine, which had overrun the north of Spain
in the sixth century and must have had many
partisans in the South of France. The violence
with which those heresies had been suppressed
had left behind it a spirit of antipathy to
ecclesiastical authority and orthodox doctrine,
which would incline the people to give at least an
attentive hearing to the Catharist missionaries.
Other influences, favourable to the new heresy,
which were at work in that region will be dealt
with in my next chapter.

It was in Southern France that Catharism made
its supreme effort and found—for a time—its
appointed home. Elsewhere—in France north
of the Loire, in Flanders, in Germany—there were
many outbreaks of Catharism. But for the most
part they were spasmodic and sporadic. The
heresy never laid hold of the people as it did in

the towns of Lombardy and, above all, in Southern France. Indeed in some places, when there were outbreaks of it, the people were actively hostile and took upon themselves to lynch the heretics.

When the fourteenth century opened, Catharism in Western Europe was either dying or dead. It lived longer in its birthplace—the Balkan Peninsula. In Bosnia, in particular, it defied all the efforts of the Popes to dislodge it; and it was not till the Turks appeared on the scene, that it finally passed away.

CHAPTER II

THE TRAGEDY OF LANGUEDOC

IT was in Southern France, especially in that part of it which I shall call Languedoc,[1] that Catharism won its greatest and most enduring triumph. There, as I have said, a higher degree of civilization and culture was reached, in the days of the Roman Empire, than in any other western province; and in the " Dark Ages " which followed the fall of the Empire the torch of civilization and culture burned more brightly there than elsewhere. And with enlightenment came contempt for superstitions, such as those which the Latin Church had taken over from

[1] The land of the heretics stretched from the Italian Alps to the west of the upper waters of the River Garonne. It was bounded on the south by the Mediterranean Sea and the Pyrenees. There has never been any one name for that region. I propose to speak of it, loosely and somewhat inaccurately, as *Languedoc*. The noun *Languedoc*, like the adjective *Provençal*, has both a wide and a narrow range of meaning. My excuse for using it to designate the land of the heretics is that the *langue d'oc* was spoken in all parts of that land and that the district which was afterwards known as the province of Languedoc was, with Toulouse, the chief theatre of the Albigensian crusade and the consequent wars.

the people and incorporated in its own system, aversion from religious bigotry, and impatience of ecclesiastical control. The position of Southern France made its seaport towns important entrepôts for commerce; and the exchange of goods was accompanied, as so often happens, by an exchange of ideas which made for mobility of mind and freedom of thought. This and the higher culture of the people gave rise to a spirit of tolerance which distinguished Languedoc from other parts of Christendom. The Jews were not only exempt from persecution, but were allowed to take part in the social and economic life of the community, and were employed by the nobles and even by the bishops as administrators of their finances and managers of their estates. Enriched by commerce and industry they acquired unwonted power and influence. In Narbonne alone there were nearly 300 Jewish houses; and in that and other towns the synagogue took its place, openly and fearlessly, by the side of the Christian church. Where Jews could be tolerated and even welcomed, a Christian heresy might well hope to find favour and support.

The whole of Languedoc swarmed with warlike counts and barons who fought incessantly among themselves. Many of these held their lands by allodial rather than feudal tenure;

and feudal discipline—a feeble influence at the best—played but a small part in the political life of the country. At the beginning of the thirteenth century the sovereignty of the Counts of Toulouse was recognized by about half of Languedoc; but their direct authority counted for less than the influence of their court, which was famous for its patronage of art and letters and its extravagance in dress and fashion. The life of the nobles seems to have been free, careless, joyous, lax in morals, polished in manners, and distinguished by a vivid and widespread interest in culture, as the word was understood in those days. The troubadours, or poets of Southern France and the adjacent regions, belonged for the most part to the noble class, and no fewer than twenty-three of them were reigning princes. " There were also troubadours," says Saintsbury, " who made song their profession and who wandered from castle to castle and from bower to bower. Both classes exercised a social influence which was most remarkable. They had great privileges of speech and censure, entered into questions of politics, and, above all, created around the ladies of the court an atmosphere of cultivation and amenity which nothing had hitherto paralleled." [1] They sang of the joys rather than the

[1] *Encyclopædia Britannica*, Eleventh Edition.

sorrows of life, and when Languedoc fell upon evil days they gradually ceased to sing.

In the towns, enriched by commercial enterprise and manufacturing industry, proud of their municipal independence, which may have been, in part at least, a survival from the days of Imperial Rome, the burghers imitated the manners of the nobles, and rivalled them in extravagance of dress, in chivalrous courtesy, in martial ardour and in devotion to art and song. Their commerce brought them into touch with the whole Mediterranean world. They had constant intercourse with the Saracens of Palestine and the Moors of Spain; and from their commercial ventures they brought back, as did the nobles from the Crusades, new ideas, new ways of living and of looking at life, and an interest in other religions than their own. They were also impatient of episcopal domination, and they shared with the nobles sentiments of hostility to the Church and contempt for its priesthood.

This free-and-easy society—rich, cultured, independent in spirit, impatient of authority, open-minded to the verge of free-thinking, tolerant of foreign ideas, beliefs and practices, tolerant of, and even friendly to the (elsewhere) despised and persecuted Jews—was a seed-bed admirably prepared for the reception and propa-

gation of heresy. Even if the Catholic Church
had won the affection, and its clergy the esteem,
of the people, it would have been difficult to
exclude heretical influences from the Italian
passes and the seaports of Languedoc, and still
more difficult to prevent the wide diffusion of
those influences. But the Church had forfeited
the affection of the people, and it is scarcely an
exaggeration to say that the clergy were generally
disliked and despised. The worldliness, avarice
and ostentation of the bishops deprived them of
spiritual influence, with the result that their
secular power was resisted and their secular
authority not unfrequently defied. The ignorance, superstition and immorality of the parochial
clergy exposed them to hatred and contempt.
Instead of saying, by way of protest, " I would
rather be a Jew than do so and so," it was
customary in Languedoc to say, " I would
rather be a *curé*," etc.

In their irregular lives and their neglect of
their official duties the *curés* seem to have
followed the example set them by their ecclesiastical superiors. Achille Luchaire, in his *History
of Innocent III*, gives a long list of abuses which
were forbidden to bishops and abbots by Church
councils held in Southern France, and adds
that " in this list we have a picture of the
morals and manners of the time." The admis-

sions of the monkish chronicler, Geoffrey de Vignier, the sarcasms of some of the troubadours, the charges contained in letters written by Innocent III, all point to the same general conclusion. After detailing in one of his letters some of the simoniacal practices of the bishops, the Pope goes on to say : " Thence comes the insolence of the heretic, thence the contempt of the nobles and the people for God and his Church." Of the Archbishop of Narbonne he says : " This man knows no God but money, and has a purse in place of a heart. In the ten years of his arch-episcopate he has not once visited his province or even his own diocese. When a benefice is vacated he keeps it vacant so that he may appropriate its revenues. With the same end in view he keeps in his own hands archdeaconries as they fall vacant, and has reduced by half the number of Canons of Narbonne. In his diocese monks and regular canons unfrock themselves, marry,[1] become money-lenders and take to various secular pursuits."

The great, and often misused, wealth of the Church in the Middle Ages excited the cupidity of the nobles, who were ever ready to dispute

[1] " Marry " is perhaps a somewhat euphemistic translation of the French words *prennent femmes*. One would like to know what were the Pope's *ipsissima verba*.

its titles to its possessions, and to make good,
by force or fraud, their claims to its lands and
other sources of revenue. Nowhere was the
feud between the Church and the nobility so
bitter or unintermittent as in Languedoc. And
as the clergy had forfeited the esteem of the
people, the nobles felt that they could oppress
them with impunity. And, to make matters
worse, they were exposed to the attacks of
bands of brigands, by whom, owing to the lack
of a strong central government, the countryside
was infested, who regarded the churches and
monasteries, with their many treasures, as fit
objects of their predatory violence, and whose
excesses were winked at, if not actually en-
couraged, by the anti-clerical nobles.[1] Nor
were the nobles and the brigands the only
despoilers of the Church. The burghers in the
towns had won municipal independence, in part
at least, at the expense of their ecclesiastical
overlords, and had frequent feuds with the
latter.

Such was the state of things in Languedoc

[1] Some of these brigands, or *routiers*, were mercenaries
in the pay of the warlike counts and barons. One of the
demands made upon the Count of Toulouse by the Papal
Legate in 1204, was that he should disband and expel
from his country the *routiers* in his service, who were
mercenaries from Navarre and Basque-land. In those
lawless times disbanded mercenaries would probably
take to brigandage on their own account.

when it was invaded in the early years of the eleventh century by the Catharist heresy. Some of the exponents of the heresy were missionaries pure and simple. But on the whole it may be said to have travelled, as revolutionary ideas and beliefs have so often done, along the highways and byways of commercial intercourse. In Southern France, with its manufacturing industries and its active trade both by land and sea, it must have found many opportunities for propagating itself among the people. So rapid was its progress that by the middle of the twelfth century it seems to have become the dominant religion of Languedoc.

For this there were many reasons. The nobles welcomed it as a powerful ally in their quarrels with the Church. For though it called itself Christian and claimed to be the only true exponent of Christian doctrine, it was in open revolt against the authority of Rome. The Waldensians, who had many adherents in Languedoc, tried to reform the Church from within by advocating a return to primitive beliefs and practices. The Catharists attacked it from without. Neither the nobles nor the burghers were shocked by their heretical doctrines, for in that brilliant society tolerance in matters of religious belief was carried so far as to be scarcely distinguishable from free-thinking.

But what of the demands which Catharist doctrine made on those who believed it? The lords of Languedoc were by no means models of virtue or even of propriety. Many of them were loose livers. Irregular warfare and lawless love seem to have been two of their chief pastimes. The striking contrast between the laxity of their morals and the rigorous asceticism which the Catharist *perfecti* preached and practised, may well make us wonder what attraction that austere heresy could have had for men of such easy virtue. But they had been taught by the religion which they professed that supernatural grace, if duly communicated by an accredited agent, could wipe out the sins of a lifetime, and not only procure a free pardon for the sinner, but also make him, by a miracle of transformation, just, holy and acceptable to God; and they may well have felt that if this was so, if supernatural grace, fraught with such possibilities, could be transmitted from God to man, the channel of transmission ought at least to be clean; and the contrast in this respect between the purity, the austerity and the single-mindedness of the Catharist ministers, and the immorality, the worldliness and the negligence of too many of the Catholic clergy must have impressed them deeply and raised to a high power the admiration which even the libertine can feel for ascetic austerity and disinterested devotion. Under the influence of this feeling the tolerance which had always been one of their virtues may well have transformed itself into active sympathy and made them ready to welcome the new religion, to countenance its teaching and to support and protect its missionaries and ministers. The exponents of the Catharist faith did not expect the rank and file of mankind to reach the impossibly high standard which their own example set them, but they themselves did at least practise what they preached.

The multitude must have been attracted partly by the virtuous lives of the *perfecti*, partly by their charitableness, and their care for the poor, the sick and the afflicted. The name which the *perfecti* habitually bore—*les Bonshommes*, the good, kind men—shows how highly they were esteemed by the people and indicates one of the sources of their influence. And rich and poor alike may well have been attracted by a theology which, instead of threatening them with an eternity of torment in a quasi-material hell, or even with a temporary sojourn in the cleansing fires of purgatory, told them that the earth on which they lived was hell and purgatory in one, that they could, if they would, escape from it at death, and that in the fulness of time all men would be saved.

How deeply the heresy was rooted in the affection of the people is proved by the reluctant admission of a champion of orthodoxy. For ten years (1205–1215) St. Dominic laboured among the heretics of Languedoc trying to win them back to the " true faith." Following the example of the ascetic *perfecti*, he " travelled over the country on foot and barefooted, in extreme poverty, preaching and instructing in highways and villages and towns, and in the castles of the nobility, controverting and discussing with the heretics." [1] He made but few converts, and in his last sermon he admitted the failure of his efforts : " For many years I have exhorted you in vain, with gentleness, preaching, praying and weeping. But, according to the proverb of my country, where blessings can accomplish nothing blows may avail." He then threatened his hearers with violent measures and warned them of the calamities that awaited them.

The threat and the warning came too late. Long before they were uttered, a storm, violent beyond measure, had burst over Languedoc. But let us go back to the twelfth century. So rapid was the growth of the Catharist sect that it was able to organize itself as a church. In the latter half of the century we find Southern France divided into five bishoprics, in all of

[1] *Encyclopædia Britannica*, Eleventh Edition.

which absolute dualism reigned supreme. The
Catholic bishops and lower clergy, whether from
indifference or from consciousness of their
impotence, offered but a feeble resistance to the
spread of the heresy. Such opposition as it
encountered drew its inspiration from the region
north of the Loire. An anti-heretical council
held at Tours in 1163 was followed in 1165 by
a half-hearted movement against the heretics
on the part of the southern bishops. Persecution was not to be thought of. To invite the
Catharist leaders to a public discussion on
points of doctrine was as far as the bishops
presumed to go. In response to a summons
from Girald, the Catholic bishop of Albi, many
of the bishops, princes and leading nobles of
Southern France assembled for this purpose at
the castle of Lombes near Albi. There they
were met by the Catharist leaders, who demanded
that a free discussion should take place and that
the umpires should be chosen equally from the
two parties. Both these demands were reluct-
antly conceded. In the course of the discussion
the Catharists threw off all disguise and openly
denounced the Catholic clergy as ravening wolves,
seducers, hypocrites, lovers of this world's
honours and goods. Gaucelin, Bishop of Lodève,
condemned their doctrines as heretical; and
his sentence was approved by the bishops and

nobles who were present. But no measures
were taken against the Catharist leaders. Nor
did the condemnation of their doctrines shake
in any degree the allegiance of the people to
their *Bonshommes*. On the contrary, the Catholic
clergy did but realize their helplessness in the
face of a movement which had the support of
popular sympathy and was protected by the
prevailing spirit of tolerance. And the Catharists, far from being discouraged by their experi-
ences, held a church council of their own two
years later at Caramen, near Toulouse, which
was attended by Nicetas, Bishop of Constantinople, and Marcus, Bishop of Lombardy, and in
which measures were taken to delineate the
boundaries of certain Catharist bishoprics. No
attempt was made to interfere with this council,
which was held openly and in complete security.

Ten years later Raimond V, Count of Toulouse,
who was at war with some of his neighbours
and wished to secure the support of the Church
in his quarrel, came forward as a defender of
the Catholic faith. As the sympathies of his
own subjects were with the heretics, he invoked
aid from without. He appealed to the Pope
(Alexander III) and to the Kings of France
and England. As the result of an understanding
between the Pope and the two kings, a mission
was sent to Toulouse, composed of sundry

E

bishops and preachers, under the direction of
the Papal Legate, Peter of Parma. The mission
was ill received by the people of Toulouse, who
listened with but scant attention to the preaching of Henry, Abbot of Clairvaux. It was then
resolved to make an example of one of the
leading heretics. Peter Moran, one of the
richest and most highly respected citizens of
Toulouse, whose zeal for Catharism had won
him the title of John the Evangelist, was summoned before the tribunal of the mission.
Threatened with the confiscation of his worldly
possessions, he recanted, and did penance in
public, and made amends in other ways for his
error. Other notable heretics followed his
example and made their peace with the Church;
but the people of Toulouse were exasperated
rather than intimidated by the proceedings of
the mission.

After this doubtful success, the Abbot of
Clairvaux was sent into the region of Albi and
Carcassonne, where the heretics were under the
protection of Roger, Viscount of Béziers and
Carcassonne. Roger retired into the mountains, leaving his wife and children in the castle
of Castres, and in his absence was declared a
traitor, a heretic and a perjurer, and duly
excommunicated. But the net result of the
mission was a few isolated recantations—" *un*

résultat à peu près nul," said one of the members of the mission, the Abbot of Mont St. Michel.

Three years later Alexander III made a fresh attempt to put down the heresy. The Abbot of Clairvaux, who had recently been appointed Cardinal Bishop of Albano, was authorized to preach a crusade against the heretics and to raise an armed force to accompany him in his mission. For the first time in the history of Christendom a Papal Legate directed military operations against Christian heretics. The castle of Lavour, one of the strongholds of the Viscount of Béziers, in which some of the Catharist leaders had taken refuge, was captured after a brief siege and the surrounding country cruelly devastated. One of the Catharist leaders was killed and two recanted. The Viscount of Béziers abjured the heresy in order to obtain peace, and some of his nobles followed his example. That was the net result of this " foretaste of the Babylonian woe." The people, in spite of their sufferings at the hands of the invaders, remained faithful to the *Bonshommes ;* and the Viscount, in spite of his nominal abjuration of heresy, continued to favour it and to protect the heretics. In 1194 Raimond V, Count of Toulouse, who had persecuted the heretics, died, and his son, Raimond VI, who was friendly to them, succeeded him. Decrees against the heretics which had been passed by the Councils of Verona (1184) and Montpellier (1195) were not followed up. The Pope, Celestine III, was engaged in a quarrel with the Emperor, Henry VI, which took up all his time and thought. And Catharism in Languedoc had never been so formidable as when his successor, Innocent III, ascended the Papal throne.

This masterful Pope was not a religious bigot. Indeed, he seems to have been more of a lawyer than a theologian, more of a statesman than a zealot for the faith. Nor did he favour violent measures against heretics, except as a last resource. He began by advocating and even practising methods of persuasion. But he was solicitous for the unity of Christendom; and the spectacle of a nominally Christian country in almost open revolt against the spiritual authority of Rome, and of the heretical poison which had produced this result diffusing itself throughout the length and breadth of Christendom, was one which he could not tolerate. He saw that the chief cause of the spread of heresy was the misconduct of the Catholic clergy, in all their grades—their worldliness, their avarice, their immorality, their neglect of duty; and he set to work to reform the more flagrant of the existing abuses. Nothing bears more eloquent witness to the widespread demoralization of the

clergy than the earnestness with which he insists
in his pastoral letters that the unworthiness of
the officiating priest no more interferes with the
efficacy of the sacraments which he administers
than the ill-health of a physician would interfere
with the efficacy of the drugs which he prescribed.[1]

But the reform of abuses which were widespread and of old standing was bound to take
time. Meanwhile heretical Languedoc must at
all costs be brought back into the Catholic fold.
Soon after his accession to the pontifical throne
and again in 1207, Innocent drew up a list of
measures which were to be taken against the
heretics. They were severe measures, but less
severe than those which princes and bishops and
mobs had already spasmodically taken. Im-
prisonment, banishment, confiscation of property,
deprivation of the rights of citizenship, refusal
of Christian burial, were among the penalties
to be inflicted, but there was no mention of
the extreme penalty of death. In regularizing
the proceedings against heretics Innocent did
to some extent mitigate their severity. In

[1] A feeble argument, to which the ancient saying
" Physician, heal thyself" is a fair rejoinder. It is
notorious that the personality of the physician has ever
been a potent influence in the treatment of his patients.
There is a counter argument from analogy which the
heretics of the day might well have advanced: Water
which is carried through corroded pipes becomes tainted
in transit.

certain cases, as in his dealings with the tyrannical
Bishop of Auxerre, he allowed appeals against
unjust and lawless action, summoned the accused
to Rome and appointed special tribunals to
investigate the charges brought against them.

For the first ten years of his pontificate
Innocent strove to extirpate heresy by semi-
pacific methods. He sent legates to superintend
the carrying out of the measures which he
ordained—foremost among whom were Peter
de Castelnau, from the Abbey of Fontfront,
(appointed in 1203) and Arnauld Amalfric,
Abbot of Citeaux (1204)—and armed these
legates with plenipotentiary powers. In 1204
he transferred jurisdiction in matters of heresy
from the bishops to the legates, and so laid the
foundations of the all-powerful tribunal which
was afterwards known as the Inquisition. He
even conferred on the legates the right to
deprive unworthy clerics of their benefices and
to fill the vacancies at their good pleasure,
without delay and without allowing an appeal.
By these measures the legates were transformed
into autocrats who could do as they pleased
in matters of clerical discipline in the lands
which they entered. But it was one thing to
have unlimited powers and another thing to
be able to exercise them. In 1204 the intrepid
Castelnau wrote to the Pope, admitting the

failure of his efforts and asking to be allowed to return to his cloistered life. But the Pope urged him to persevere.

The task which had been set him was, however, one of extreme difficulty. Apart from the disrepute into which the Church had fallen and the widespread sympathy of the people with the heretics, the Papal mission had to encounter an almost insuperable obstacle in the political anarchy which reigned in Southern France, and in the consequent absence of any central authority with whom the legates could deal. The leading prince was Raimond VI, Count of Toulouse. Innocent tried to win him over. Celestine III had excommunicated him, not for having favoured the heretics but for having harried the monasteries. Innocent absolved him on the understanding that he would take measures against the heretics and cease to harry the monasteries. He promised to do both these things, but did neither. A year later he was denounced to Rome by the Abbot of St. Gilles and was then formally required to send away the irregular troops who were in his pay and who seem to have been little better than brigands, and to expel the heretics from his dominions. Again he made facile promises and again he broke them. The fact is that it was practically impossible for him to keep them. The semi-brigands who were in his pay—mercenaries from Navarre and Basque-land—were his only attempt at an army; for where there was no feudal discipline feudal levies could not well be raised. And had he expelled the heretics and their supporters he would have deprived his country of the greater part of its inhabitants, both urban and rural. In fine he was being asked to commit political suicide, and he found it easier to promise to do so than to keep his word.

In 1207 Castelnau, despairing of obtaining satisfaction from Raimond, tried to induce the nobles to leave off fighting among themselves, to sign a general peace and to form an anti-heretical league. Raimond was invited to join the league, but he refused, for he felt that it was really directed against his people and himself. He was then excommunicated and his own domain was placed under an interdict—a measure which was approved by the Pope, who launched an anathema against him and wrote him a letter full of bitter reproaches and couched in violent terms. The Count yielded to this pressure and, having renewed the promises which he had so often broken, was duly absolved by the Pope.

But the Pope now realized that it was useless to invoke his aid in the campaign against the

Catharists. To whom could he turn for support? Of the Southern princes there were only two on whose loyalty he could at any time have counted with full assurance—William VII, Lord of Montpellier, and Peter II, King of Aragon, and overlord of Béziers and Carcassonne. But the Lord of Montpellier died in 1202, and was succeeded by his daughter, whom the King of Aragon married for the sake of her estates; and the King of Aragon, whose sister was married to the Count of Toulouse, and who was by no means disposed to take up arms against his brother-in-law, proved a broken reed. The Catholic prelates, immersed for the most part in worldly affairs, took but a half-hearted interest in the campaign against the heretics and secretly resented their subjection to the authority of the Papal legate.[1] The burghers were heretics at heart, and the multitude were devoted to their *Bonshommes*.

It was clear that Languedoc would not of itself expel the poison of heresy from its system. In 1206, the legates, more downhearted than ever, spoke of resigning their office. On the 17th of November, 1206, the Pope ordered them to try another method. They were to choose

[1] Three of the bishops had to be deposed and their sees filled by loyal Catholics. One of the latter, Fulk, Bishop of Toulouse, played a leading part in the anti-Catharist crusade.

men of proved virtue and religious zeal, and
send them out, as Christ sent out his disciples—
on foot, poorly clad, living austerely—in the
hope of converting the heretics, by example as
well as by preaching and disputation, from the
error of their ways. In taking this step, the
Pope, who was not above being taught by his
enemies, may well have had in mind the successes which attended the missionary labours of
the austere Catharist *perfecti* and humble Wal-
densian preachers.[1] In itself, whatever may
have been its immediate result, the step was a
most momentous one, for to it we owe the
inception of the Mendicant movement which
played so great a part in the history of Latin
Christianity. But so far as the conversion of
the Catharist heretics was concerned it was
ineffective. It may, however, be doubted
whether the method of peaceful persuasion

[1] In 1209 Innocent authorized a band of missionaries,
bearing the title of " Poor Christians," under the leadership of one Durand of Huesca, to combat heresy in
Languedoc and elsewhere. These " Poor Christians "
were Waldensians, whose outspoken criticism of the
Church and zeal for reforming it had exposed them to
the charge of heresy, and who had then made their peace
with the Pope and entered his service. Dominic's
mission to the heretics—see p. 63—seems to have been
undertaken on his own initiative, and that of the Bishop
of Osma. But the " Poor Christians " were undoubtedly
forerunners of the mendicant monks, and Innocent's letter
to the legates in November 1206 was the real starting
point of the whole Mendicant movement.

which the Pope prescribed ever had a fair trial, for barely fourteen months after it had been inaugurated Castelnau, the Papal legate, was assassinated, and the war-clouds which had long been gathering, precipitated by this senseless crime, broke in all their fury over Languedoc.

The war-clouds had long been gathering; for even while the Pope was trying milder measures he was preparing to appeal to force. Towards the end of 1207 he renewed an appeal which he had made three times to Philip Augustus, the French King, to constrain the nobles and burghers of Languedoc to take strong measures against the heretics. The Pope was under an illusion as to the power of the French King. In effect he was King of only a part of Northern France. His suzerainty over the South was purely nominal. This was one reason why he turned a deaf ear to the Pope's appeal. Another reason was that he was at war with our King John. The appeal which the Pope made towards the end of 1207 was addressed not only to the King but also to his chief feudatories, and in general to all the nobles and knights in his kingdom. It was a solemn and urgent appeal which guaranteed to all who should take up arms the same remission of sins which was enjoyed by those who fought in the Holy Land. In reply Philip pointed out that he was at war

with the King of England and could not afford
to put two armies in the field. He was ready to
respond to the Pope's appeal, but on two con-
ditions, neither of which (as he knew well) could
possibly be fulfilled. John was to be muzzled
for two years, and the cost of the expedition
was to be defrayed in large part by the Church.
While negotiations between the King and the
Pope were in progress Castelnau was assassinated
by some underling of the Count of Toulouse.
Was the Count responsible for this crime?
Probably no more—and no less—than was
Henry II for the murder of Becket. But the
crime was one of those events which change the
face of history.

The party in the Church in favour of extreme
measures now got the upper hand. A fifth
appeal to the French King was again met by a
virtual refusal. But, with or without the support of the King, the Pope was determined that
the Crusade against the heretics should go forward. Finding that all the advantages which
attached to service against the infidel in the
Holy Land could be enjoyed at far less risk and
far less expense by service against the heretic
in Languedoc, the nobles and knights of Northern
France, and even to some extent of North-
Western Germany, responded with extraordin-
ary enthusiasm to the summons from Rome.

Again and yet again the Pope appealed for the
support of the French King; for he foresaw that
without his leadership the crusade might easily
degenerate into a war of plunder and massacre.
But as the support was not forthcoming, the
Pope took into his own hands the control and
direction of the crusade.

Had Southern France been united it might
well have repelled the invasion from the North.
Its disunion which, as we have seen, was chronic,
was its undoing. While the war-clouds were
gathering, the Count of Toulouse asked his
nephew, the Viscount of Béziers and Carcassonne, to make common cause with him against
the enemy. Meeting with a flat refusal and
being unwilling to pose as the champion of
heresy, he determined to bend before the storm.
His ambassadors, who were already at the
Papal Court, were instructed to tender his submission and to ask for some legate other than
Arnauld of Citeaux—of whose implacable stern-
ness he complained to the Pope—to be sent to
Toulouse to arrange about terms. The Pope
lent a seemingly favourable ear to his request.
In the absence of Arnauld, who was superin-
tending the preparations for the Crusade, Milon,
a notary of Latran, was sent to Toulouse as
legate. The Catholic extremists reproached the
Pope for consenting to treat with such a monster

of perfidy and dissimulation as the Count. The Pope replied in a remarkable letter, in which he unfolded his plan of campaign. "Divide and conquer" was the principle on which he proposed to act. The submission of the Count was to be accepted on terms which, without driving him to desperation, would detach him from the other "satellites of Anti-christ" and reduce him to comparative impotence. The lesser princes could then be crushed in detail; and when that had been done the Count could be dealt with according to his deserts. The terms to which the Count had to submit, though the Pope seems to have regarded them as unduly lenient and therefore as only provisionally valid, were both humiliating and harsh. He had to do penance in public, to surrender seven of his castles, to disband and banish his mercenaries, to bind himself by solemn vows to do many things which he would find it difficult if not impossible to do, to treat as heretics all persons who were denounced to him as such by the clergy, to refer all complaints that might be made against him to the decision of the legates, and—last, but not least—to join the crusading army, in other words, to take part in an expedition, the object of which was to devastate his own country and plunder and massacre its inhabitants. He was no longer the ruler of his own country. He had to all intents and purposes handed over the government of it to the Papal legates.

Meanwhile the Crusaders were marching southward. The Pope had made a last appeal to the French King to associate himself with the Crusade—to send his son Louis, if he could not go himself; but as the King now had to deal with the Emperor Otho as well as with his inveterate enemy, King John, he was able to plead, with some show of reason, that he could neither go in person nor spare his son. In his absence the army was placed under the supreme control of Arnauld, the Papal legate, whose impersonal hatred of heresy and personal hatred of the Count of Toulouse made him the life and soul of the Crusade.

But what pretext had the Crusaders for invading Languedoc? Toulouse was the headquarters of Catharism; and its Count had not only made his peace with Rome, but had also undertaken to put down heresy in his own dominions. No doubt there were other princes who protected the Catharists; but the most influential of these, the young Viscount of Béziers, finding himself isolated by the submission of the Count of Toulouse, repaired to Montpellier and tried to come to terms with the Legate. His overtures were rejected. Had his submission been accepted the Crusade would have lost its *raison d'être*. Arnauld had made up his mind to strike terror into the heretical South. The Viscount took counsel with his vassals, and determined to take up arms against the invaders. Leaving a strong garrison in Béziers, he threw himself, with the *élite* of his knights, into his chief stronghold, Carcassonne. Béziers was stormed by the Crusaders, its inhabitants were massacred without regard to age or sex, and the town was pillaged and burnt. Before the massacre began the Legate was asked how the Catholics were to be distinguished from the heretics. He answered, " Kill them all : God will know his own." [1] From 15,000 to 20,000 persons are said to have perished, including 7,000 who had taken refuge in the church of St. Mary Magdalen.

The fall of Béziers had the desired effect of striking terror into the surrounding country. Narbonne submitted and, as a propitiatory sacrifice, put some heretics to death. The Crusaders, taking possession *en route* of many abandoned castles, moved on to Carcassonne. The siege began on August 1. Chanting their favourite war song *Veni Creator Spiritus*, the

[1] Doubt has been cast on this story, but Schmidt, in a footnote to Vol. I. p. 229 of his History, gives reasons for regarding it as well authenticated.

crusaders assaulted and captured the suburbs. The inner fortress defied them. But it was a hot summer. The wells were drying up; and the sufferings of the inhabitants were great. Taking advantage of this Arnauld invited the Viscount to come and discuss terms of capitulation. The Viscount consented in order to save the lives of his people. On arriving at the camp he was treacherously detained as a prisoner. The bulk of the inhabitants fled, leaving all that they possessed behind them. Of those who were captured 50 were hanged and 400 burned alive as heretics. The Viscount was imprisoned in his own palace, where he died shortly afterwards, " *miserabiliter interfectus.*" The town was pillaged, but not burnt. The Legates apologized to the Pope for not having treated it as they had treated Béziers. The interests of the crusaders had to be considered. Had the town been destroyed it would have been impossible to lodge and feed the army.

After the fall of Carcassonne the army began to break up. The barons from the North, who had fulfilled their vows and earned their indulgences, wished to return to their own domains. What was to be done with the conquered country? If it was not to relapse into heresy, a ruler must be found for it whose orthodoxy was above suspicion. Arnauld summoned the

F

leading nobles to a conference and offered the fiefs of Béziers and Carcassonne in succession to the Duke of Burgundy, the Count of Nevers and the Count of St. Paul, by all of whom the offer was indignantly rejected. They had come south, they said, to chastise the heretics, not to usurp domains to which they had no title. What these nobles refused, almost as an insult, Simon de Montfort, Earl of Leicester, a noble whose religious zeal was only equalled by his secular ambition, after some show of resistance, accepted.

The great army now broke up. Some of the crusaders, actuated by fanaticism, or cupidity, or perhaps—like their leader—by both motives, remained behind and took service under de Montfort; but the majority returned to their own homes. In order to find funds for the maintenance of his army, de Montfort appealed to the Pope, who helped him to the best of his ability, but unfortunately had another crusade —that against the Turks—to finance. Such help as he was able to give enabled de Montfort to maintain a force which, though much smaller than the crusading army, was better disciplined and more fanatical.

The time had come for the Count of Toulouse to be dealt with. The Papal legates, supported by the Bishop of Toulouse, and other bigoted Catholics, wished to depose him. De Montfort

wished to annex his territory and his title.
But as he had made due submission to Rome
pretexts had to be found for the hostile action
which was contemplated. The loyalty of his
subjects, orthodox as well as heretical, had to
be reckoned with; also, the support which he
received from his brother-in-law, the King of
Aragon; and, above all, the interference of the
Pope, who was now disposed to protect him and
safeguard his sovereign rights as long as he
posed as a loyal son of the Church. The legates
played their cards with consummate skill and
with an unscrupulous disregard of existing
agreements and obligations. By ignoring the
spirit of the instructions which they received
from Rome, and putting their own interpretation
on the letter of them, they were able to manœuvre
both the Pope and the Count into false positions,
which brought them into conflict with one
another against the will of each. They presented the Count with a series of extravagant
demands which he could not have complied with
without delivering himself, bound hand and
foot, into their power. His refusal to comply
with these demands, which they had no doubt
foreseen, was treated as a *casus belli ;* and the
legates took upon themselves to excommunicate
and depose him. Having driven him to take up
arms in self-defence, they were able to denounce

him to the Pope as a champion of heretics and a
rebel against the Church; and the Pope, accepting their version of what had happened, endorsed
the extreme measures which they had taken.

The struggle which ensued lasted for nearly
twenty years. Fortune inclined first to one
side, then to the other. De Montfort, who was
a brave and skilful warrior, won many successes
in the field, and at one time was on the point
of realizing his ambition; but he was killed in
1217 when besieging Toulouse, and his son and
heir, Amaury, was not the man to carry on his
father's work of conquest or to found the dynasty
of which his father had dreamed. He could
make but little headway against the forces which
the Counts of Toulouse, father and son, were
able to array against him. Raimond VII, who
succeeded his father in 1222, was more fortunate
in the field than the latter had been. But, like
his father, he was under the ban of the Church,
and, unlike his father, he had to contend against
the armed strength of the French monarchy,
which had now stepped in to reap what others
had sown. Exhausted by the protracted struggle,
he made peace with his enemies in 1229. He
had to undertake to suppress heresy in his own
dominion, and, in order to make the suppression
effective, he had to allow the Inquisition to be
established in Toulouse and other towns. And

he had to become the vassal of the French King, whose shadowy suzerainty was now turned into substantial sovereignty.

Meanwhile the unhappy land which had been the theatre of the crusade and the war that followed it, had suffered untold misery. Wherever the Catholic leaders carried their arms, massacre, plunder, confiscation and general devastation went with them and famine and pestilence stalked behind. When the Castle of Minerve was starved into surrender, 140 *perfecti* who had taken refuge in it were captured and given their choice between recantation and the stake. Only three recanted. When Lavaur was taken (1211) Amalric de Montréal and eighty knights were hanged. But the gibbet, hastily erected, gave way beneath their weight, and de Montfort gave orders for their throats to be cut. The commandant's sister was thrown into a well, and there was the usual holocaust of *perfecti*. There was another such holocaust when the Castle of Casser surrendered, for of the sixty *perfecti* who were taken not one recanted.[1] All went cheerfully to the stake.

---

[1] Peter des Vaux de Cerni, the historian of the Albigensian war, describes the " extreme joy " with which the crusaders burnt and tortured the heretics. The cup of their joy must have been full when a stronghold surrendered, and full to overflowing when a batch of *perfecti* fell into their hands.

These were not isolated cases. " Each forward move," says Achille Luchaire, " on the part of the invading army was marked by a butchery." Had the counsels of the legates and the more fanatical prelates and monks been followed the war would have been one of absolute extermination. When de Montfort began the siege in which he was killed, the legates exhorted him, in the event of his taking Toulouse, to put all its inhabitants to death. When Amaury de Montfort, aided by Prince Louis, captured Marmande, the Bishops of Béziers and Saintes urged the Prince to hand over the inhabitants to Amaury so that the latter might burn or hang them all. The Prince refused; but in spite of his refusal, the soldiers of Amaury forced their way into the town, where, under orders from the Bishop of Saintes, they butchered more than 5,000 men, women and children.

Where there was such scant respect for life, respect for property was not to be looked for. Confiscation, plunder and pillage were the order of the day. The army lived in large measure on the country which it devastated; and it was self-interest, not clemency, which restrained the soldiers from the wholesale burning of villages and crops. As it was, there was much wanton destruction, for the inhabitants had to be terrorized as well as chastized.

When a war of aggression is waged with flagrant disregard of humanity and justice, there are sure to be fierce reprisals. From time to time the people of Languedoc were goaded into acts of extreme violence, and Catholic historians have made much of these. But if the violence which is born of desperation is to be condemned, what are we to say of those who provoked it by driving the people to despair? When there is an equal exchange of atrocities the chief blame must rest with the original aggressors. But in the Albigensian wars the exchange was not equal. For each act of reprisal there must have been at least fifty wrongs to avenge.

When Raimond VII made peace with his enemies his country had suffered much. But a worse fate was in store for it. For it was now to come under the harrow of the Inquisition. We have seen that the Albigensian crusade degenerated, under the guidance of Arnauld and de Montfort, into a war of worldly ambition. Innocent, who rightly resented this unforeseen change of direction, thought to mend matters by declaring in a letter to the legates, that the crusade was " off." If, as seems probable, he was under the impression that Catharism had been suppressed, he was entirely mistaken. Catharism had not been suppressed. It outlived the crusade by more than a century. And though it died at last, it was not killed by persecution. Its death, so far as it was due to external causes, was an indirect rather than a direct result of the crusade.

However erroneous may have been the doctrines of the Catharists, the steadfastness with which they endured persecution and the pertinacity with which, in the face of untold dangers and difficulties, they carried on their spiritual activities, prove the sincerity of their convictions. Innocent III who, in keeping with the spirit of his age, identified heresy with abandoned wickedness, accused them of hypocrisy, and historians who ought to have known better have repeated the charge. There is no foundation for it. Again and again the Catharist ascetics and ministers, in fifties and hundreds, were given their choice between recantation and a cruel death. Unhesitatingly, and even joyfully, they chose the latter. They may almost be said to have thrown themselves into the flames. Not one per cent. recanted. Hypocrisy is not made of such stern stuff as that.

When the storm of persecution was at its worst some of the Catharist leaders fled to other countries; but the bulk of them remained in Languedoc, finding shelter in distant strongholds, in mountains and forests and caverns, and in general in remote and inaccessible haunts. There they kept in touch, as far as was possible, with their flocks, holding services at midnight and in secret places, and visiting the sick and dying under cover of darkness. Whenever there was a rift in the clouds they returned to their posts and resumed their interrupted minis- trations. The hold which they had on the affections of the people was too strong to be easily shaken. The severity of the measures which were taken against them throughout the whole of the thirteenth century, is a tribute to their power and influence. In the third decade of that century, when the star of Raimond VII was in the ascendant, they held their heads almost as high as they had done before the great crusade.

Hence the need for the Inquisition. It was in the struggle against Catharism that the Inquisition, as an organized institution, came into being and assumed the form with which the student of mediæval history is familiar.[1] Finding that princes and prelates, even when reinforced by papal legates, could make but little headway against the heretics, Pope Gregory IX in 1232 transferred all inquisitorial

---

[1] In the thirteenth century, especially in France, Catharism was heresy *par excellence*. The words *catharist* and *heretic* were almost synonymous.

powers to the order of mendicant monks which
St. Dominic [1] had recently instituted; and
though in France efforts were made from time
to time to bring these inquisitors under the
control of the bishops, the mendicant monks
won the day and constituted themselves the
supreme authority in the matter of maintaining
purity of faith. Placed by the rules of their
order outside the social life of the community,
alien to its interests, hostile to its spirit, inaccessible to all considerations which might have
weighed with local inquisitors (whether lay or
clerical) and inclined them to clemency, the
mendicant monks became the most rigorous and
implacable of heresy-hunters. They thus came
to be regarded by the Holy See as a militia
devoted to its interests and ready to fight on
its behalf, and they obtained from it a succession of privileges which were so many encroach-
ments on the authority of the bishops, the
functions of the priesthood and the rights of
the secular power. Being directly subordinated
to the Pope, who alone instituted them and
could alone revoke their commission, they were
accountable to him alone for the discharge of

[1] A few years later the same powers—and privileges—
were conferred on the Franciscans. The two mendicant
orders, which in their origin were essentially evangelistic,
seem to have been rivals in their eagerness to be used
as the instruments of tyranny and terrorization.

their duties, and except to him there was no appeal against their judgments.

To secure convictions as speedily as possible, and by whatever means, seems to have been the chief aim of the Inquisition. The Council of Narbonne in 1233 decreed that the adverse testimony of witnesses should be regarded as conclusive, in spite of the most strenuous denials on the part of the accused. It further decreed that convicted criminals and other scoundrels should be admitted as *hostile* witnesses. The supporters, the followers, the servants, the children of accused persons could bear witness against them, but not for them. And as pecuniary rewards, as well as indulgences, were offered to those who denounced heretics, and as personal enmity and other base motives might well weigh with those who came forward, and as unwilling witnesses could be put to the torture, the difficulty of securing a conviction was reduced in every case to the barest minimum. But other precautions were taken by the Inquisition. The accused were not allowed to confront their accusers, whose names were carefully withheld from them. They could not defend themselves, nor appeal against sentences of condemnation. Magistrates, advocates and notaries were forbidden under pains and penalties to assist them in any way; and the Councils of Valence (1248) and Albi (1254) decreed that those who offered to depose in their favour were to be regarded as supporters of heresy. Thus from first to last the dice were heavily loaded for the prosecution and against the defence. To be accused was virtually equivalent to being condemned.

Condemnation for heresy involved confiscation of all property, both real and personal, deprivation of all civil rights and liability to death at the stake. Heretics who voluntarily recanted had to do penance, rigorous and humiliating, for the rest of their lives. Heretics who recanted under compulsion were liable to be imprisoned for life in solitary cells or even in subterranean dungeons. And various disabilities, both ecclesiastical and civil, were inflicted on the descendants of heretics.

The measures against heresy decreed by the Church could not have been carried out without the support of the State. How was this secured? By threats and bribes. The prince who protected heretics or was even lukewarm in suppressing them ran serious risks. He could be excommunicated by the Holy See. His country could be placed under an Interdict. His vassals and other subjects could be absolved from their allegiance to him. And foreign princes could be invited to wage war against him. The

Counts of Toulouse learned all this to their cost. But it was chiefly by bribery that the Church secured the support of the secular power. The money raised by the confiscation of the property of heretics and the fines inflicted on their supporters were divided in various ways. Some of it went to the upkeep of the Inquisition. Some, as rewards for delation. Some was assigned to the diocese. Some to the commune. But the greater part, at any rate in France, went into the coffers of the State. And as long as heresy-hunting was a source of profit to the Crown, the work of the Inquisition could go forward without let or hindrance.

Of the work of the Inquisition in Languedoc during the thirteenth century, Paul Daniel Alphandery, Professor of the History of Dogma at the Sorbonne, writes as follows : "The chronicle of the inquisitor, Guilhem Pelhisse (d. 1268), shows us the tragic episodes of the reign of terror which wasted Languedoc for a century. . . . The inquisitors played the part of absolute dictators, burning at the stake, attacking both the living and the dead, confiscating their property and their land, and enclosing the inhabitants both of the town and of the country in a network of suspicion and denunciation. The secular authorities were of the utmost assistance to them in this task; owing to the

confiscations the Crown had too direct an
interest in the success of the inquisitorial trials
not to connive at all their abuses. Risings
against the inquisitors were followed by terrible
measures of repression. In May 1242 the
inquisitors and their agents were massacred
at the castle of Avignaut.[1] This massacre led
to a persecution which went on without opposition and almost without a lull for nearly fifty
years. Appeals to the kings of France and the
Popes had but little effect. A moment of hope
at the beginning of the fourteenth century was
followed by a fresh movement of repression
carried out by the inquisitor Bernard Guy
(1308–1323)."

If the storm of persecution then abated, it
was for want of victims, for Catharism in Southern
France was on its death-bed. It was not the
Inquisition that was killing it. It was dying of
the mortal malady which it had brought with
it into the world—dying of the dualistic philosophy which it shared with Christianity, but
which it both carried out to its logical conclusion
and made the cardinal dogma of its creed.
Christianity has tried to escape from some at
least of the logical consequences of dualism.

[1] Two years later the Castle of Montségur, the chief
stronghold of Catharism, was captured. Two hundred
perfecti were found in it, who were all burnt alive by the
inquisitors without even the formality of a trial.

It has not succeeded. Dualism is still, as it has ever been, its evil genius. But the attempt has so far saved it from the doom of the religion which not only accepted the more paradoxical of those consequences but even proclaimed them to the world as " saving truth."

Catharism would have died in any case. The breath of free inquiry which was beginning to move on the face of the waters would sooner or later have proved fatal to it. The Inquisition may have accelerated its death. But the chief external cause of its decline was the infiltration of Northern blood, Northern influences and the Northern outlook on life into the South. The knights and nobles from the North whom the crusade had introduced into Languedoc and who had settled there in the lands and castles of their dispossessed owners, intermarried little by little with the old nobility, till at last a fusion of the two races and even of the two languages—the *langue d'oc* and the *langue d'oil* (or *d'oui*)—began to take place in the upper strata of Southern society. While this fusion was being effected the South was gradually losing its distinctive character and beginning to merge its individuality in that of France. This brought the upper classes under the influence of the French Crown—which, for political and economic, if not for religious, reasons, was strongly anti-heretical—and also of the ideas which dominated society in the region north of the Loire. The lower classes in Languedoc, so far as they were heretical, were thus deprived of the support and sympathy and protection of the upper; and though they strove, with touching fidelity, to maintain contact with their spiritual leaders, even when the latter had been driven into the forests and mountains, to receive their ministrations, and in return to give them help and succour and the means of living, the strain upon their resources, if not on their loyalty, was too great. Little by little they went back into the fold of the Church which had given them good reason to fear and hate it.

And so Catholicism triumphed in Languedoc. But at what a cost! Persecution may ensure conformity to the letter of a religion, but by its base appeal to fear and greed, and by its implicit demand for hypocrisy and mendacity, it kills the religious spirit. And the religious spirit is the spirit of life. The culture of the South—its regard for art and letters—in which it had given a lead to Christendom, was dying or dead. The tolerance which had come with its superior enlightenment, and which was out of place in an age of bigotry and violence, had proved its undoing. The troubadours, oppressed by the gathering gloom, had ceased to sing. " Song," said the last of them, " should express joy, but sorrow oppresses me, and I have come into the world too late." The joyousness, the light-heartedness of the old *régime* had given place to lamentation and mourning and woe. Meanwhile the systematic encouragement of spying and delation was demoralizing the people, and the " network of suspicion and denunciation " in which they were enclosed was as fatal to their economic as to their social life.

Peace reigned at last. But was it worth what it had cost? *Solitudinem faciunt. Pacem appellant.* Peace reigned in the land; but it was the peace, not of reconciliation and goodwill but of destruction, desolation, despair and death.

This was the virtual, though not the actual, end of Catharism. Its survival for another century in Bosnia no more affected its general decline than the retention of ebbing waters in a sea-pool affects the general recession of the tide. When it died out in Languedoc it had, to all intents and purposes, passed away.

It had passed away; but it had not lived in vain. For one thing, it had given to the world one of those splendid examples of loyalty to a cause and constancy in affliction which from time to time revivify our flagging faith. No

G

martyr to a spiritual conviction has ever died more heroically than those whom the crusaders and the inquisitors consigned to the flames. In other respects its influence outlived it. The Church which persecuted it to the death learned much from it. " The influence of Catharism," says F. C. Conybeare, " on the Catholic church was enormous. To counteract it celibacy was finally imposed on the clergy, and the great mendicant orders were evolved; while the constant polemic of the Cathari teachers against the cruelty, rapacity and irascibility of the Jewish tribal God led the Church to prohibit the circulation of the Old Testament among laymen. The sacrament of ' Extreme Unction ' was also evolved by way of competing with the death-bed *consolamentum*." [1]

One way of combating an enemy is to study his methods and meet him, if that should seem desirable, with his own weapons and his own tactics. The Church adopted that policy in its struggle with Catharism; and in order to carry it out it had to begin to reform itself. It was to the example of austere and simple living with which the Catharists and their fellow-heretics, the Waldensians, enforced their protest against the wealth and worldliness and consequent corruption of the Church, that the

[1] *Encyclopædia Britannica*, Eleventh Edition.

Mendicant movement owed its inception; and the Mendicant movement gave the Church a new lease of life. For this, if for nothing else, the Church owed, and still owes, the heretics a debt of gratitude, which it has ill repaid by its incessant efforts to blacken their memory. But we are apt to hate those whom we have injured; and the Church finds it hard to forgive the heretics for the atrocities which it inflicted on them.

CHAPTER III

THE PHILOSOPHY OF CATHARISM

To oppose Catharism to orthodox Christianity, as a dualistic to a non-dualistic religion, is a complete mistake. Christianity is monotheistic, Catharism, ditheistic. This is a legitimate distinction. But in spite of, or perhaps because of, its monotheism, Christianity is dualistic to the core. What Catharism did was to accept the dualism which is at the heart of Christianity, as of every religion which had its spiritual home in Western Asia, to carry this out into its logical consequences and so to reduce it to a practical absurdity.

Monotheism, so far as it dissociates itself from pantheism, is necessarily dualistic. The distinction between the Creator and his creation, with the derivative distinction between the Supernatural and Nature, goes down to the very foundations of the universe. It goes deeper still. Its depth is unfathomable. It assumes that the universe has no foundation except in the will of One who is entirely outside it, who (in the words of Catholic theology) " is distinct from it really and in essence."

And its dualism, besides being unfathomably deep, is all-pervading. It takes a thousand forms and meets one at every turn. This is true more especially of the doctrine, the policy and the practice of the Church of Rome, the arch-champion of the dualism which separates the Creator from the creation, God from man. " Rome," says Professor Gwatkin, " never overcame the false dualism of God and man, in which divine and human stand apart, or are connected only by some definite divine action. Latin thought always tended to regard God's action as abrupt and definite, and his revelation as a series of miraculous interventions breaking through the order of a sinful and transitory world. They stand out like points of brilliant light, but the rest is utter darkness, for there is no diffused light in the Latin sky. God acts every now and then with a high hand and outstretched arm; but the rest of the world almost goes its way as if there were no God. The authorities of the Church were constituted once for all, the faith was delivered to them once for all. . . . What more could be wanted? No salvation but by grace; and grace was the gift of an absent King to the one visible Church, a remedy applied externally to individuals through the sacraments which the Church dispensed on such terms as it thought fit. This false dualism of God and man carried with it a false dualism of sacred and profane in public and private life. The Church was not only separated from the State, but in time sharply opposed to it as to something essentially profane. . . . There is the same divorce of sacred and profane in private life, the same refusal to recognize a revelation in the common experience and intercourse of mankind. Certain persons, places, times and things are supposed to be sacred in themselves, or rather made so by the Church, while others are essentially common. Thus in the case of persons there is the contrast of priests and laymen; of places, that of chancel and nave; of times, that of the saints' day and the common day. All these, and still more conspicuously the Latin doctrine of the Lord's Supper are samples (to quote Dr. Hort) ' of the unbelief which ascribed a life-giving power to visible things because it assumed the heaven and the earth to be divided by an impassable chasm.' So too the contrast of the ' religious ' life and the ' secular.' " [1]

And this all-pervading dualism takes forms other than those which Professor Gwatkin has

[1] *The Knowledge of God*, Vol. II.

noted. Thus, in logic, we have the dualism of
being and *non-being*, as set forth in the Law of
Contradiction—a law which governs the course
of things as well as of thought and which even
controls the action of God. " The creation of
matter," says a Catholic theologian, " must have
been instantaneous, because there is no medium
between existence and non-existence." [1]

In psychology, we have the dualism of soul
and body, a distinction which interposes an
impassable chasm between man and the rest
of the animal world. It might be contended
that the higher animals had at least the rudi-
ments of souls. But a dualistic psychology for-
bids such an hypothesis. A soul is a thing
complete in itself. You have it or you do not
have it. Man has it; and he can therefore be
lost or saved. The beasts cannot have it, or
they too would be candidates for heaven or
hell. As they are soulless, man has no moral
obligation to them, " no more than to stocks
or stones." [2]

In morals, we have the dualism of mortal
and venial sins. It is not easy to see where the
line between these is to be drawn. But there
is a line, or rather there is a profound abyss.
For venial sins are easily atoned for and for-

[1] *Outlines of Dogmatic Theology*, by Fr. S. J. Hunter, S.J.
[2] *Moral Philosophy*, by Fr. Rickaby, S.J.

given, whereas a mortal sin, if not washed away
by supernatural grace, dooms the sinner to an
eternity of separation from God. He who dies
in mortal sin is a lost soul.

As regards man's spiritual condition, there is
the dualism of justification and reprobation,
of the friendship and the enmity of God. Each
of us is at any given moment in a state either of
justification or of reprobation, which means that
if he died in that moment he would either be
saved or lost. And so complete is this dualism
that the transition from state to counter-state
is always (like the creation of matter) instantaneous.

Beyond the grave this dualism reproduces
itself in the appalling abyss between heaven and
hell, between an eternity of bliss and an eternity
of misery. One or other of these alternatives
is the doom of each one of us except, indeed,
of the infant who dies unbaptized, for whom
(somewhat illogically) an intermediate state
called *limbus* has been found.

The plain truth is that, as a conscious thinker,
the average man is incurably dualistic, and that
he stamps his dualism on the creeds which he
controls. " Yes *or* No " is the question which
he is ever asking, and to which he expects a
prompt and straightforward answer. " Yes *and*
No " is, in his eyes, the answer of the sophist,

the shuffler or the coward. In the Near East
the philosophy of religion—the *official* philosophy—came under his control long ago and
has remained under it ever since. In India,
which has never had a dominant official creed,
the philosophy of religion has eluded his heavy
hand. In the solitude of their forests, detached
from the workaday world in which men are
being ever tempted and even constrained to
take sides, the sages of the Upanishads, medi-
tating on the supreme problems of existence,
saw that the world was one, not two. A fundamental protest against dualism has been India's
contribution to the higher thought of mankind.
And the protest has remained a protest and is
strong to-day because it is still a protest. No
facile system of monistic thought has been
generated by it, to rule men's minds for a time
and then crystallize into dogma and die. Or if
there have been such systems, the protest has
outlived them all; for no scheme of thought,
no formal creed, can meet its demand for all-
embracing unity, and so silence its insistent
voice.

If Catholic Christianity, true to the spirit of
its birthplace, is dualistic through and through,
why is Catharism to be blamed for having made
dualism the central feature of its creed? Before
we can answer this question we must find out

where and how Catharist dualism broke away from that of the Church. This quest will not long detain us. It was in its attempt to solve the problem of the existence of evil that Catharism departed from the Catholic tradition and went its own way. Given that the world in which we find ourselves is the handiwork of a Supernatural Person of infinite power, wisdom and goodness, how are we to account for the evil which defiles and disfigures it?

"What, did the hand then of the potter shake?"

If it did not, when and where and how did things go wrong?

Various answers have been given to this question. There is the fatalistic answer which, while accepting the simile of the clay and the potter, boldly affirms that the hand of the potter did *not* shake, that on the contrary it fashioned evil as carefully and as deliberately as it fashioned good. This is the solution of the problem which has found expression in such familiar texts as " I form the light and create darkness : I make peace and create evil : I the Lord do all these things," and, " The Lord hath made all things for himself : yea even the wicked for the day of evil "; and which has generated the fatalism of the Mussulman and the predestinarianism of the Calvinist. And there is the ultra-optimistic answer which denies the reality of evil, affirming that evil is only " good in the making," or again, that

" The evil is null, is nought, is silence implying sound."

Neither of these answers will satisfy those who are in the grip of evil; and, though both may be in keeping with the hypothesis of creation through evolution, neither is in keeping with the hypothesis of direct and final creation by a Being whose power, wisdom and goodness are all infinitely great. If there is any meaning in the word *good* when applied to God, the fatalism which regards God as the author of evil, is an implicit denial of his goodness. And the optimism which admits the actuality of evil in the very act of denying its reality, is an implicit restriction of the degree and scope of his power.

The third solution of our problem is that which the Christian Church took over from Judaism. According to the story of the Fall, the world as God created it was " very good "; but an act of disobedience on the part of the first man and woman brought evil into it—the moral evil of sin and sorrow and the physical evil of disease and suffering and death—and has infected it with evil ever since. The only thing to be said for this, the orthodox explanation of the existence of evil, is that under the deadening influence of authority and custom—each in its way a narcotic to the mind—it has been un-critically accepted as adequate ever since it began to be dogmatically taught. Or rather it had been so accepted until Darwin set men thinking and led them to ask it for its credentials. Its foundations have now been undermined. When it is critically examined its inadequacy resolves itself into absurdity. On the face of it, it is a myth and nothing more. As a myth it has its meaning and its value. Taken literally and seriously, it has one deadly flaw. It im-pugns all the supreme attributes of God. The Creator, whose created work could be com-pletely deranged and demoralized by a single offence committed by two of his creatures—an offence which must have been foreseen and may almost be said to have been provoked—is neither all-mighty, nor all-wise, nor all-good.

The truth is that the problem, *as it is stated by supernatural religion*, is insoluble. The Super-natural Person, who could call a world into being, into the very fulness of its being, by the fiat of his will, and who was in himself absolute perfection, could not have created an imperfect world. In the act of creating such a world he would have proved to demonstration that his power, or his wisdom, or his goodness was less than infinite. If we admit the reality, or even the actuality, of evil, we must abandon the orthodox conception of creation; and in doing so we must admit the inadequacy of the orthodox conception of God.

Catharism had its own solution of the insoluble problem. It carried the dualism which is inherent in the terms of the problem to its logical conclusion. It denied that a perfect God could have created an imperfect world; and, admitting the reality of evil, it contended that whatever is evil must have had an evil source. For the dualism of the Creator and the created world, it substituted the uncompromising dualism of two Creators, two acts of creation, two created worlds. In other words, it gave full scope and a free rein to the disruptive potentiality of dualism. It rent the Universe asunder, and interposed between the two dissevered worlds an abyss which in strictness could neither be fathomed nor spanned.

But how was evil to be distinguished from good? In the world of our experience the two are freely intermingled. What is the distinguishing mark, the " note " of each? The Catharist was at no loss for an answer to this question. Matter is intrinsically evil. Spirit is intrinsically good. The world of the good God is the world of spirits. The world of the bad God is the world of material things. How,

then, are we to account for the presence of
spirits on earth? According to the fundamental
hypothesis of Catharism, the two worlds have
nothing whatever in common. Yet man, as it
seems, belongs to both. A human being is a
spirit imprisoned in flesh. How did intercourse
between the two worlds become possible? Why
did the spirits that people earth leave their own
world and so come under the sway of the Evil
One?

It was in the attempt to answer these questions
that the myth of the Devil's visit to heaven was
invented. As an explanation of the tragedy of
man's life on earth that myth is not more absurd
or more inadequate than the myth of the forbidden fruit. Each myth is an attempt to
extricate speculative thought from a false
position. The myth of the forbidden fruit is
supposed to explain the presence of evil in a
world which was originally good. The myth of
the Devil's visit to heaven is supposed to explain
the presence of good—in the form of spiritual
life—in a world which is intrinsically evil.

If the Catharist solution of the problem of
evil is a greater outrage on common sense and
right reason than the "orthodox" solution,
this is due to its being the outcome of a bolder
and more logical handling of the fallacious
assumption which is common to both creeds.

The more thoroughly and consistently you develop a false conception, the more widely do you diverge from truth. If a conclusion shocks you and you can find no flaw in the reasoning process which led up to it, you may be sure that the premises from which it was deduced were unsound. Sweeping condemnation of Catharism as a " wicked heresy " carries with it condemnation of dualism in general, and in particular of the dualistic doctrine of a supernatural Creator and an aboriginal act of creation.

Catharism has been reproached for its pessimism; and it is true that it regarded earth as under the rule of the Devil, and man's life on earth as a penitential pilgrimage. But was it so much more pessimistic than Christianity, which regards the earth as lying under the curse of the sin of Adam, which thinks of the Devil as " the prince of this world " and the natural man as " the enemy of God " ? And if Catharism carried pessimism so far as to identify this world of ours with hell, it can at least be said for it that it knew of no worse hell than this; that its hell was temporal and purgatorial; that for good or for evil it was very much what man chose to make it; and that the awful shadow of eternal punishment did not fall upon the lives of its inmates.

For, whatever may be thought of their respective outlooks on this life, it must be admitted that in respect of its eschatology Catharism was far more humane than its great rival. Catholicism has always taught—and Protestantism inherited the doctrine—that God pours into the world an endless succession of souls, all of whom, as they enter the world, are under sentence of condemnation. And as nothing but an infusion of supernatural grace can avert the doom which they have incurred, and as the Church alone can dispense supernatural grace, and as five-sixths of the human race are and have always been outside the Church, and as inside the Church there are and always have been many " reprobates," it is clear that only a small remnant of mankind can be saved. But Catharism, anticipating in this respect the universalism of certain latter-day Christians, taught that in the fulness of time all men would be saved. It is true that the Catharist, like the Catholic Church, claimed that outside the Church there was no salvation. The extravagance of this claim, by whomsoever made, need not be insisted upon. But there is this difference between the claims of the two Churches, that Catharism meant by loss of salvation nothing more than another return to earth, whereas Catholicism means by it nothing less than eternal perdition, eternal separation from God, eternal suffering in the fires of a quasi-material hell.

It was to the doctrine of rebirth that Catharism owed the humaneness of its eschatology. This doctrine, which was a necessary deduction from the Catharist story of the Fall, though repugnant to Western prejudices and foreign to the spirit of official Christianity, has one great merit. There is implicit in it a gospel of " eternal hope." For rebirth provides the soul with a succession of opportunities for repentance and amendment, or—from another point of view— for self-development and self-transcendence; and it will continue to provide such opportunities till full use has been made of them; in other words (to adopt the Catharist standpoint) till the last remaining soul has finished its pilgrimage on earth.[1]

The sharp distinction which Catharism drew between the religious and the secular life ought not to have shocked the Catholics, for their Church had long emphasized the same distinction,

[1] In formulating the doctrine of rebirth, and in teaching that man, by his own action, can cut short the succession of his earth-lives, Catharism came into line with Buddhism. But the resemblance between the two religions, though striking, is purely accidental. In essence the two are at opposite poles. Catharism is the very apotheosis of dualism, whereas Buddhism inherited from the Upanishads the fundamental protest against dualism which, as we have seen, is characteristic of Indian thought.

H

and had laid additional emphasis on it when it
realized what a strong argument—strong in
effect if not in logic—for the truth of Catharist
doctrine was implicit in the austere asceticism
of the *perfecti*.

The uncompromising attitude of Catharism
towards marriage, which it condemned in un-
sparing terms even while it permitted the
" believers " to marry, contrasts unfavourably
with the wisdom of the Catholic Church, which
treated marriage as a sacrament and regarded
sexual intercourse as lawful and right when the
" intention " of those who indulged in it was
directed towards the procreation of children.
But it must not be forgotten that Catholicism
has always thought of marriage as a concession
to human weakness, and of the married state,
with its joys and cares and responsibilities, as a
distraction from the spiritual life, and that it
has always regarded celibacy as the ideal state.
And here too the Church was not above being
taught by its enemy, for its enforcement of
celibacy—in principle at least—among the clergy
of all types and grades dates from the time of
its life and death struggle with Catharism.

We now come to a matter of vital importance
in which Catharism shows to advantage as com-
pared with Catholicism, the very irrationality
of its philosophy having proved, in a sense, its

salvation. Its condemnation of matter as a creation of the Devil, as intrinsically evil, and as the source of all evil, both moral and physical, compelled it to spiritualize its conception of the administration and operation of sacramental grace, and so saved it from sinking into the slough of materialism and superstition into which sacramentalism is so apt to descend. We have seen that one of the causes of the success of Catharism as a proselytizing religion was the scandal created by the worldliness and immorality of the Catholic clergy—from highest to lowest. Many of the parish priests, besides neglecting their official duties, were living in open sin. As the Church taught that without an infusion of supernatural grace no one could be saved or even do anything that was acceptable to God, and as it also taught that the sacraments by which supernatural grace was communicated to man could not be administered by any persons except duly ordained priests, the question naturally arose : If a priest who was living in open sin administered a sacrament, would the rite be efficacious? The corrupt state of the priesthood when Catharism challenged the Catholic Church made it inevitable that the question should be answered in the affirmative. A negative answer would have been equivalent to a confession of failure on the part of the Church. Yet it was not without searching of heart that the affirmative answer was given. The letters of Innocent III on the subject make this clear. The pains which he took to prove that a bad priest could administer the Sacraments of the Church with due effect suggest that his mind was not really at rest, that he had secret misgivings which he was trying to silence. He had good cause for uneasiness. To say that the unworthiness of the minister is no bar to the efficacy of the sacrament, besides removing a strong incentive to correct living on the part of the officiating priest, opens the door to a purely materialistic conception of sacramental grace on the part of the recipient. For it is equivalent to saying that the grace of God acts mechanically, not spiritually, and that the priest is nothing but a tap which can either admit the waters of healing or shut them off. It is the weakness of sacramentalism—a weakness which is due to its dualistic origin—that in the mind of the ordinary unenlightened believer it readily degenerates into a materialism which is closely allied to the savage's belief in magic.

And the greater the stress that is laid on the sacramental side of religion, the more imminent is the danger of the machinery of religion killing the spirit of it. Not long ago the *Church Times* quoted with sympathy, if not with formal approval, the words of an Anglo-Catholic parent who said "that if he had daughters he would send them to make their first confession to a drunken priest in order that they might understand that it was not the personality of the man that mattered but his priesthood."[1] This is materialism of a gross and debased type. Indeed it comes near to being a reversion to primitive magic. A more complete despiritualization of a belief which claims to be essentially spiritual could not well be imagined. The effect on the mind of the young girl of the contrast between the disgusting state of the officiating priest and the awful solemnity of the rite which he was blindly administering, the shock which it would be likely to give to her aspiration and her faith, is entirely ignored. The "atmosphere" that invests the sacred rite counts for nothing. The outward act is the only thing that matters. We could not have a more significant example (to repeat Dr. Hort's words) "of the unbelief which ascribes a life-giving power to visible [or audible] things because it assumes the heaven and the earth to be divided by an impassable chasm."

Against this debasement of the sacramental idea the Catharists entered an emphatic protest. Its adoption by the Pope was a proof—so they

[1] Leader in *Church Times*, May 12, 1916.

contended—of the corruption of the Catholic Church. In the administration of their own sacrament, the *consolamentum,* the outward act of the minister was purely symbolic. It was his prayer alone that mattered; and if his prayer was to be efficacious his heart must be pure. He who had forfeited the gift of the Holy Spirit could not be the means of conferring that gift on others. This, though a hard saying for those who desired, in sincerity and good faith, to receive that gift, was a truer and braver solution of the problem than that which the Catholic Church found itself compelled to adopt. Yet it was not the final solution. If the unworthiness of the minister is no hindrance to the efficacy of the sacramental rite, then of two things one. Either the efficacy of the rite resides in the outward act, or the inward state of the recipient is the only thing that counts. Catharism rejected the former alternative, but did not go so far as to accept the latter. Catholicism rejected the latter—had it not done so it would have committed suicide—and, under the stress of its dualistic logic, took refuge in the former. Sacramentalists would contend that if the inward state of the recipient was the only thing that counted in the sacrament, the whole sacramental position would be undermined. And they would be right. The inward state of the would-be recipient might disqualify him for the receipt of supernatural grace, but it could not of itself insure his receiving it. Sacramentalism cannot afford to depart from the position that without the intervention of an ordained priest supernatural grace cannot be transmitted from God to man. If this assumption commits the sacramentalist to a materialistic interpretation of the sacramental idea, he must accept that interpretation as unavoidable, and, if he happens to be spiritually minded, must lean as lightly as possible on a doctrine which does not really commend itself to his higher self. The Catharist, who could not see that denial of the efficacy of the outward act, committed him, in the last resort, to rejection of sacramentalism, was less logical than the Catholic. But logic is not always the safest guide in these matters; and in his refusal to subordinate the spirituality to the machinery of religion, he was nearer to the heart of truth.

He was also nearer to the heart of truth when he contended that no one day was more sacred in the sight of God than other days, and that the meanest of meeting-houses, even though unconsecrated, might be as full of God's presence as the grandest of cathedrals. In these, and in other such matters, the very extravagance of his dualistic philosophy, by compelling him to spiritualize his religious beliefs, seems to have delivered him from some of the practical consequences of dualism.

I will now consider a feature of Catharist teaching in which, as it seems to me, the heretics were centuries ahead of the rest of Christendom. They refused to predicate goodness of the God of the Old Testament. And if he was not the good God, what could he be but the bad? In support of their position they appealed (as we have already seen) to his character as revealed in the Old Testament, and to his doings as recorded in it. We need not go into the details of their indictment of him. If one were to catalogue all the unpleasant traits in his character, and all his unjust and cruel deeds, both lists would be long.

The Catharist indictment of the God of the Old Testament was too sweeping, but the orthodox glorification of him may be said to have provoked it. It is customary nowadays to say that in the Old Testament is recorded a gradual evolution in men's conception of God, which transformed—in their minds—a tribal deity, with all the defects and limitations of the tribal outlook, into the God of the universe, a God of all-controlling power, if not of all-embracing love. This may be sound criticism, but it is a departure from orthodox teaching.

The orthodox view of the Bible is that it was fully, though not literally, inspired by God; that the various writers in it were, if not his amanuenses, at least his private secretaries; and that therefore it cannot err. To-day the inerrancy of the Canonical Scriptures is as strongly insisted upon by the Catholic Church as by any Calvinistic sect. And if the Scriptures cannot err, then, as a record of what was said and done, they must be taken quite seriously, and we must believe, without hesitation or misgiving, that all the deeds which are ascribed to " the Lord " in the Old Testament, were actually done, and that all the sayings ascribed to him were actually said, by the one and only God.

This view of the Bible in general and of the Old Testament in particular has dominated Christendom ever since the Canon of the Scriptures was framed. When I was young no one who did not wish to pass as a " freethinker " (another name for an " atheist ") would have thought of questioning it. I was brought up on Maclear's handbooks to the Bible. These books seem to be still in use. I recently took up a copy of his *Old Testament History*, and, opening it at random, read as follows : " When in the full tide of his success he [Saul] received a visit from Samuel, who bade him from God undertake an expedition against the Amalekites

and avenge the treacherous hostility which they
had shown towards the Israelites, when they
came forth from Egypt. ' Smite Amalek ' ran
the Divine commission, ' spare him not; slay
man and woman, infant and suckling, oxen and
sheep, camel and ass.' " What a Deity ! And
yet half a century ago, or less, we all believed
that Samuel's message to Saul was indeed a
" Divine commission." We all believed, quite
seriously, that God took sides in a tribal quarrel
and authorized a hideous vendetta massacre !
And Catholics and Calvinists believe it still.[1]

All honour to the Catharists for having protested against such a blasphemous misconception
of God ! Nothing has done so much to confuse
our thoughts about great matters and to debase
our moral and spiritual standards, as the orthodox
belief that all the reputed sayings and doings of
" Jehovah " were in very truth the sayings and
doings of the One authentic, all-righteous, all-
powerful God. He who believes in the creation
of the world by a Supernatural Person of infinite
power, wisdom and goodness, who believes that
the Bible is the Word of God, and who identifies
the God of the universe with the God of the Old

---

[1] When the crusaders were massacring the inhabitants
of Béziers—" man and woman, infant and suckling "—
they probably flattered themselves that they were
" smiting Amalek " and that in doing so they were
carrying out a " Divine commission."

Testament, when he finds that sayings and doings which, as judged by human standards, are profoundly immoral, are ascribed to the agency of that God, is apt to take refuge, and is indeed expected to take refuge, in the demoralizing assumption that whatever God does is right. It is to the credit of the Catharists that they refused to resort to this miserable subterfuge. The deeds of injustice and cruelty which Jehovah is said to have done, *if due to Divine agency*, were the work of omnipotent evil, not of omnipotent good. It was a bad, not a good God, who destroyed the whole human race, except eight persons, by a deluge, and who killed 70,000 Israelites by a pestilence because their king had taken a census of his people. So the Catharists protested, and there was reason in their protest. It is better to believe in a bad God, it is better to deify the Devil, than to believe that the one true God is a monster of injustice and cruelty. It is also to the credit of the Catharists that they refused to identify the jealous, vindictive God of the Old Testament with the God of the New Testament—the all-loving Father whom Christ revealed to his fellow-men—and that they regarded the latter as alone worthy of worship and devotion. It is to the confusion between the two deities, with the consequent confusion between the morality of the Law and the morality of the Gospel, the morality of literal obedience and the morality of spiritual freedom, that we owe the misunderstanding of Christ's message to the world, which has done so much to obscure the light of the Christian ideal and undermine the emancipative influence of Christianity.

The Catharists went too far when they identified the God of the Old Testament with the Devil. They lacked the literary sense which would have enabled them to appraise the Jewish Scriptures at their proper worth. Such a sense had not yet been evolved. Indeed it is of comparatively recent growth. But their application to the God of Israel of the spiritual ideal and the moral standard which Christianity owed to Christ, and their rejection of his claim to divinity because he came far short of satisfying that test, was a piece of daringly original criticism for which they deserved a better reward than persecution and death.

I cannot find anything in the Catharist heresy which warranted the extermination of the heretics. The philosophy of Catharism was no doubt unsound; but if the unsoundness of one's philosophy was a sufficient reason for sending one to the stake the whole human race would perish in one vast holocaust; for owing to the immaturity (in the present stage of his development) of man's reasoning powers and the inadequacy of the perceptive faculties which furnish reason with its data, the ultimate problems of existence are at present insoluble by human thought. And it is probable that they always will be, though it is possible that our conception of what is ultimate will be progressively and indefinitely extended.

But was the philosophy of Catharism more unsound than that of the Catholic Church? We have seen that the two philosophies had much in common. In its uncompromising dualism the Catharists carried to its logical extreme the fundamental assumption which underlies supernatural religion and which is, as I contend, its evil genius. Their division of the universe into God's world and the Devil's world is an audacious paradox; but perhaps it is not quite so violently paradoxical as it sounds. For it must be remembered that in its eschatology Catholicism ratifies that division and even perpetuates it—at man's expense. If the doctrine of eternal punishment does not mean that a large part of the human race will be handed over, finally and for ever, to the dominion of the Devil, it has no meaning. Both in Catharist and in Catholic doctrine there is a struggle between God and the Devil over the soul of man. According to Catharism the struggle with evil is a victory for God, for sooner or later all the lost souls will be restored to the heaven from which they fell. But according to Catholicism, it will be a drawn battle, God retaining his Kingdom of Heaven, while the Devil will be allowed to rule for all eternity in Hell.

The practical ideal to which Catharism was committed by its philosophy was that of extreme asceticism. This is an inadequate ideal, and I am not concerned to defend it. But it is also the *esoteric* ideal of Catholicism; and it is the ideal to which the dualism of the Supernatural and Nature necessarily directs us; for asceticism does but carry out into practice the disparagement of Nature which is implicit in the idea of the Supernatural. It is true that Catholicism has never forced the ideal on the rank and file of the faithful, and that it has never regarded the pursuit of it as a necessary condition of salvation. But exactly the same may be said of Catharism.

The sacramentalism of the Catharists, though less logical than that of the Catholic Church, was, as we have seen, simpler, purer and less materialistic. The very extravagance of their dualistic anti-materialism forbade them to attribute intrinsic efficacy to the sacramental rite, and so delivered them from the danger to which sacramentalism is always exposed—the danger of subordinating the spiritual to the mechanical side of religion and exalting ceremonialism at the expense of moral conduct and inward life.

If a tree is to be judged by its fruits Catharism might well have claimed to be a higher and purer religion than the Catholicism of its day. For such evidence as is available, including the testimony of the enemies of the Catharists, goes to show that the general level of Catharist morality was far higher than that of Catholic. This it might well be, for in that period morality in all Christian countries was at a low ebb. The Church itself set the world a bad example. The worldliness and immorality of the priesthood were among the causes which favoured the spread of Catharism and other heresies; and experience has proved that the lowering of the moral standard among those who are supposed to set a good example to the rest of the community, is at once a symptom and a cause of a general decline in morals. The Catharist ministers and *perfecti* set their followers an example of ascetic purity, self-abnegation, devotion to duty and service to others. Example is proverbially better than precept; and it would have been strange if that practical appeal to the conscience of the community had failed to influence their conduct. From all accounts the morals of the Catharists were not only high for

the age in which they lived, but would have
been considered high in any age.[1] The charge
of hypocrisy brought against them by their
enemies, who could not believe that moral goodness was possible outside the fold of the Church,
is, as I have already pointed out, a strong testimony to their moral worth.

It is high time, then, that the aspersions on
their conduct and character which have been
passed on, with the connivance of the Church,
from generation to generation, by a succession
of irresponsible historians, not one of whom had
studied the available documentary evidence,
should be withdrawn.

But slanders which have once got into circulation are not easily withdrawn. In Mrs. Webster's book on *Secret Societies and Subversive
Movements*, which was published in 1924, a
paragraph is devoted to the Albigenses, which
runs as follows : " Although not strictly a secret
society, the Albigenses were divided after the

---

[1] The worst that can be said of Catharist morality is
that in certain circumstances it sanctioned suicide.
But the circumstances were quite exceptional; and,
after all, extreme asceticism, whether practised by
Catharist *perfecti* or Trappist monks, is slow suicide;
and it is possible that the Catharist saw but little
difference in moral worth between shortening life by a
few years through prolonged and rigorous fasting and
other hardships, and shortening it by a few hours, through
abstinence from food when on one's death bed, lest, after
receiving the *consolamentum*, one should relapse into sin.

secret society system into initiates and semi-initiates. The former, few in number, known as the *Perfecti*, led in appearance an austere life, refraining from meat and professing abhorrence of oaths or of lying. The mystery with which they surrounded themselves won for them the adoring reverence of the *Credentes*, who formed the majority of the sect and gave themselves up to every form of vice, to usury, brigandage and perjury, and, while describing marriage as prostitution, condoning incest and all forms of licence." Why the Albigenses should come into a book on secret societies, I do not know, for no heretical sect ever went out more boldly into the open. Mrs. Webster's account of them is a tissue of slanderous misstatements, made (apparently) on the authority of Michelet, an erratic historian, who in this case has been content to repeat the current libels on the heretics, instead of investigating the charges against them by studying the documents that bear on the subject. As a contribution to history the paragraph is matter for ridicule rather than for serious criticism. Charges of brigandage [1] brought

---

[1] If the Catharists ever took to brigandage it must have been in sheer desperation, when they and their country had been ruined by massacre, pillage, confiscation, and in general by the ravages of persecution and war. The *routiers* who plied their nefarious trade in the days before the crusade, and whom Michelet

I

against persons who seem to have been as peaceable and industrious as Quakers, of perjury brought against persons of whom an enemy said " they neither lie nor swear," of incest (and " all forms of licence ") brought against persons who regarded sexual intercourse as sin, and marriage as a concession to human frailty, may safely be trusted to refute themselves. But the paragraph is worth quoting as an example of the way in which historians (or those who posed as such) in all ages, following one another like a flock of sheep, have maligned the helpless Catharists. It is no paradox to say that history has persecuted their memory as cruelly and as vindictively as the Church persecuted their souls and bodies while they were still in the flesh.

Why did the Church persecute the Catharists so cruelly and so vindictively? Throughout this chapter I have been asking myself this question, and by a process of exclusion I have now arrived at the answer to it. There was nothing in their teaching or their manner of living to justify the war of extermination which was waged against them. The Church persecuted them because they had committed what in its eyes is the sin of sins, the sin for which

---

probably had in mind, were not Catharists. Many of them were disbanded mercenaries who had been imported from the Basque country and Navarre.

there is no forgiveness. They had defied its authority, rejected its teaching and in general thought and acted for themselves. In a word, they were *heretics*. They had gone their own way. They had left the fold. This was enough, and more than enough, to damn them. No matter what they taught or how they lived, the fact that they thought and acted for themselves ensured their condemnation. And the calumnies of which they were the victims were a natural sequel to their condemnation. The familiar saying, " Give a dog a bad name and hang him," admits of being " converted." The Church hanged the dog for disobedience, and then, in order to justify itself in the eyes of the world, gave him the worst of bad names. And it did this so effectively that the world, ignorant of the real facts, has ever since applauded its action.

The suppression of spiritual freedom by war, persecution and other violent methods is a natural outcome of the dualism which divides the Supernatural world from Nature and believes that intercourse between the two worlds can be carried on only from the far side of the intervening abyss. For this means that if God is to reveal his will to man and order man's goings, he must select special instruments for the purpose. And this again means that he must intervene in human affairs and take sides in human quarrels. We must expect him to side with his deputies and servants—with the people whom he has chosen, with the Church which he has commissioned. Their enemies are his enemies. Whoever attacks them attacks him. Whoever rebels against them rebels against him. And as his deputies and servants are as human as the rest of us, they will be tempted to exploit his favour, in their own interests, to the full. Their personal enemies will be regarded as his enemies, and will be dealt with accordingly. Their desires, their passions, their self-seeking instincts will be solemnly dedicated to his service. Their crimes will be so many acts of obedience to his will. Their cruelties and their treacheries will be so many proofs of their loyalty and their zeal. " No faith is to be kept with heretics " because a heretic is a rebel against God. In other words, lies are to be told, solemn promises broken, and the ordinary rules of morality violated *ad majorem Dei gloriam*.

It is to this tendency of self-interest, whether individual or collective, to insinuate itself into religious zeal that we owe the wars and persecutions which, in the name of religion, have played so sinister a part in the history of Christendom and Islam, and in which millions of lives have been sacrificed and untold misery inflicted on the survivors. The God who takes sides outrivals Moloch in his demand for human victims. And he does worse than this. He confuses our ideas of right and wrong, obscures our ideals, debases our standards and demoralizes our lives.

If rebellion against the chosen instruments of the Supernatural God is a mortal sin, rejection of their teaching, disbelief in their dogmas, is of all mortal sins the most deadly. The idea of a supernatural revelation through the medium of special instruments carries with it the idea of orthodoxy in doctrine. The supernatural God communicates to his chosen instruments, for the benefit of mankind, the ultimate truth of things, or so much of this as it is fit for men to know; and the truth which is thus communicated is duly set forth in catechisms and creeds. But here a difficulty arises. The words which men use to express their knowledge or their vision of high realities, say different things to different persons, mean different things in different ages, and in general are in a state of flux and transition. Also, as there are many languages, we can never be sure that a certain word in one language has the same shade of meaning as the corresponding words in other languages, and conveys exactly the same idea to all who use it? How, then, is ultimate truth, when it has been received from God, to be formulated? And what is the value of formulas which convey different shades of meaning (however slight the differences may be) to different minds? The Church of Rome met, or rather evaded, this difficulty in two ways; by its use of Latin, a dead language, a language which has ceased to change and grow, and by its claim to determine the exact meanings of the words that are used in theological exposition or religious controversy. " If the Church," says Fr. Hunter, S.J., " could not define words with infallible precision, how could it teach? " How indeed? Their use of the mother tongues of the various peoples whom they proselytized was one of the causes of the success of the Catharists; and it was also one of the most heinous of their sins. The " orthodox " solution of the language difficulty is, on the face of it, an absurdity. Anyone who has ever reflected on the laws and properties of words and has realized how they change and pass and wax and wane, and take colour from their contexts, and even from the minds of those who use them, will laugh it out of court. But it was no laughing matter for the heretics who broke away from the Church on points of doctrine. It was for disbelief in the teaching of the Church, more than for any other offence against its authority, that men languished in dungeons or died at the stake. How men lived, how they bore themselves in the ordinary affairs of life, how they conducted themselves in their dealings with one another, were matters of minor importance. Correct belief was the thing that mattered most. " This is the Catholic faith, which except a man do keep whole and undefiled, without doubt he shall perish everlastingly." The echo of these words has been heard in every age; and, as long as the Church had the power to persecute, it took care that before a heretic perished everlastingly he should have a bad time in this temporal life.

Such are some of the consequences of the doctrine of a supernatural revelation and the sub-doctrine of a supernaturally guided Church. A doctrine which has borne such poisonous fruit is obviously unsound, and the philosophy which is behind it is obviously inadequate. It is our dualistic thought which has misled us, and we must now try to find a more trustworthy guide. The world is one, not two. In its unity there is infinite multiplicity and infinite variety. The range of its being from pole to pole is infinite, but there is no break in it, such as that between the Supernatural and Nature, no unfathomable abyss with a phantasmal world on each side of it—phantasmal because it has been robbed of reality by its divorce from the other world, which is not so much its alternative as its counterpart and (in a sense) its other self.

What form recognition of this fundamental truth will take and what form religion will take when the truth has been recognized I cannot pretend to say. To define the relation of man to Ultimate Reality is and will ever be beyond the power of human thought; for Ultimate Reality recedes as we approach it, and retires to higher and higher planes of being, as we climb to higher and higher levels of imaginative thought. When men have realized this, and have convinced themselves that they cannot by searching find out God, and that dogmatism is the arch-enemy of faith, the quest of God will perhaps take another direction and, having escaped from the tyrannical control of conscious thought and from the fallacies of its inadequate logic, will work itself out in our hearts and our lives.

And the nearer we get to the heart of truth the more tolerant we shall become. Intolerance is generated, in part at least, by secret self-distrust. We persecute dissentient opinion because its existence makes us doubtful—though we will not admit this—of the truth of our own convictions, because we resent its challenge to our faith. None are so tolerant as those who really know; and the reason is that no amount of dissentient opinion can affect, even by a single vibration, the stability of belief which has transformed itself into knowledge. While men are still theorizing they are apt to quarrel and lose their tempers; but when a theory has been fully tested and has taken its place as a truth of science, its advocates are well content to wait, in the calmness of complete assurance, for its final acceptance.

Tolerance may be the outcome of indifference; if it is, it is as negative and as futile as its source. This is not the tolerance of which I am thinking. I am thinking of the tolerance which is vigorous and active, which springs from recognition of the manysidedness of truth and the inadequacy of human thought, which measures the strength and serenity of faith, which expresses itself in sympathy and understanding, and is near of kin to the charity which St. Paul exalts. The more there is of that spirit in the atmosphere that surrounds us, the better it will be for the world. It is by way of an appeal to it that I have retold the story of the Albigenses. The intellectual honesty and independence of the heretics, the sincerity of their convictions, the earnestness of their desire to serve God and live up to their faith in him, their capacity for self-sacrifice, the ascetic purity of their lives, the constancy with which they endured persecution, the courage with which they faced death, were qualities which a wise Church would have tried to utilize for good, and which it was criminal folly to persecute to the death. To realize this, to realize that the story of the dealings of the Church with the heretics is a shameful chapter in history, to realize, in this case if in no other, the madness and the wickedness of religious persecution, and the fundamental falsity of the philosophy which countenances and even necessitates such action, will be a step in advance. For it will be a stage in the growth of the spirit of true tolerance; and the growth of that spirit will be both a sign and a cause of a nearer approach to truth.

PRINTED IN GREAT BRITAIN BY RICHARD CLAY & SONS, LIMITED,
BUNGAY, SUFFOLK.